Gooseberry Patch Co.®

Jolly Holidays

A Country Store In Your Mailbox®

Gooseberry Patch
600 London Road
Department Book
Delaware, OH 43015

★

1·800·854·6673
gooseberrypatch.com

Copyright 2002, Gooseberry Patch 1-888052-97-X
First Printing, April, 2002

How To Subscribe

Would you like to receive
"A Country Store in Your Mailbox"®?
For a 2-year subscription to our 96-page
Gooseberry Patch catalog, simply send $3.00 to:

Gooseberry Patch
600 London Road
Delaware, OH 43015

Contents

Dedication

To all of you who still love little red wagons under the tree, plump sugar cookies, glittery gumdrops and the first sparkly snow of the season.

Appreciation

For sharing your warmest memories and all of your recipes that are just right for celebrations, we thank you.

Friendship Soup Mix

Cyndy Rogers
Upton, MA

A hearty and delicious gift when delivered with a loaf of freshly baked bread...tie it all up in a new kitchen towel!

1/4 c. dried split green peas
1/4 c. dried split yellow peas
1/4 c. pearled barley
1/2 c. dried red lentils
1/4 c. dried, minced onion

2 t. Italian seasoning
1/2 c. long-grain rice, uncooked
1/2 c. elbow macaroni, uncooked

Layer ingredients in the order listed in a one-quart, wide-mouth jar; attach instructions.

Instructions:

Remove macaroni from jar and set aside. Brown one pound ground beef or turkey; drain. Spoon into a large stockpot; add 3 quarts water, one, 28-ounce can of diced tomatoes, undrained, and remaining soup mix. Bring to a boil; reduce heat. Cover and simmer for 45 minutes; add macaroni. Cover and simmer 15 to 20 minutes longer or until vegetables are tender. Makes 16 servings.

It is in giving that we receive.
- St. Francis of Assisi

Snowman Soup

Sandra Renaux
Orlando, FL

*A sweet & simple gift for kids
and kids at heart!*

1-oz. pkg. hot cocoa mix
1 candy cane

2 T. mini marshmallows
1 milk chocolate drop

Place ingredients in a plastic zipping bag; attach instructions.

Instructions:

Santa says you've been good this year...
I'm always glad to hear it!
With freezing weather drawing near,
You'll need to warm the spirit.
Here's a little snowman soup,
Complete with stirring stick.
Add hot water and sip it slow...
it's sure to do the trick!

Don't wait until Christmas Day
to use those festive holiday
dishes...keep 'em out all season
long for a daily dose of cheer!

Apple Cider Spice Mix

Annette Ingram
Grand Rapids, MI

For a welcome hostess gift, fill a basket with a jug of apple cider,
cider mix, mugs, coasters, oranges and a bunch of
cinnamon sticks tied up with a pretty ribbon.

2 c. sugar
2 t. cinnamon
1 t. ground cloves

1-1/2 t. allspice
1/4 t. nutmeg

Combine ingredients together; store in an airtight container. Attach instructions. Makes about 24 servings.

Instructions:

Heat one cup cider until hot but not boiling; stir in 2 teaspoons cider spice mix until dissolved. Pour into a serving mug; garnish with a cinnamon stick and slice of orange.

Make picking out the tree a family tradition...enjoy
warm cider and homemade doughnuts
after the snowy walk through the woods!

Raspberry Hot Cocoa Mix

Sharon Tillman
Hampton, VA

The combination of chocolate and raspberry make this mix heavenly!

2 c. powdered sugar
1 c. baking cocoa
1 c. non-dairy powdered creamer
1/2 t. salt

3 .15-oz. pkgs. unsweetened
    raspberry drink mix
5-1/2 c. powdered milk

Combine ingredients together in a gallon-size plastic zipping bag; shake to combine. Place in an airtight container; attach instructions. Makes 9 cups of mix.

Instructions:

Add 3 tablespoons mix to one cup of hot water; stir until dissolved.

Tie freshly baked gingerbread cookies to your Christmas tree
with festive ribbon...give one to each holiday guest
for a sweet treat after dinner.

Banana-Nut Bread in a Jar

Audrey Lett
Newark, DE

Makes a great gift for friends & neighbors...home-baked goodness!

2/3 c. shortening
2-2/3 c. sugar
4 eggs
2 c. bananas, mashed
3/4 c. water
3-1/3 c. all-purpose flour
1/2 t. baking powder

2 t. baking soda
1-1/2 t. salt
2 t. cinnamon
1 t. ground cloves
2/3 c. chopped pecans
8 1-pint wide-mouth canning
    jars and lids, sterilized

Cream shortening and sugar together; blend in eggs, bananas and water. In another mixing bowl, sift flour, baking powder, baking soda, salt, cinnamon and cloves together; mix into banana mixture. Fold in nuts; mix well. Pour into well-greased jars, filling each 1/2 full; wipe rims clean. Set on a baking sheet and bake at 325 degrees for about 45 minutes; wipe rims again. Put on lids; set on counter until lids ping which means a seal has been made. Sealed jars may be stored in a cool, dry place for up to 6 months; unsealed jar contents should be eaten or kept refrigerated for up to one week. Makes 8.

Host an ornament exchange this year and use clear ornaments for invitations! Use a paint pen to write the date, time and place...be sure to pack them carefully before sending.

Spice Cake in a Jar

LaVerne Fang
Joliet, IL

These handy little cakes make easy teacher gifts
and they're always a big seller at our church bake sale!

2/3 c. shortening	1 t. cinnamon
2-2/3 c. sugar	2 t. baking soda
2 c. applesauce	1/2 t. baking powder
4 eggs	2/3 c. chopped nuts
3-1/3 c. all-purpose flour	2/3 c. raisins
1-1/2 t. salt	8 1-pint wide-mouth canning
1 t. ground cloves	jars and lids, sterilized

Mix first 10 ingredients together; fold in nuts and raisins. Spray each jar with non-stick vegetable spray; fill each 1/2 full with batter. Bake at 325 degrees for 45 minutes; remove jars from oven and immediately put on sterilized lids and rings. Set aside to cool; when lids ping, jars are sealed properly. Cake has a shelf life of 6 months. Makes 8.

There are no bells in all the world so sweet
as sleigh bells over snow.
-Elizabeth Coatsworth

PB&J Muffin Mix

Carol Burns
Gooseberry Patch

*Arrange this yummy mix in a gift basket along with
a jar of peanut butter and a jar of fruit jelly.*

1-1/2 c. all-purpose flour
2 t. baking powder
1/2 t. salt

1/2 c. cornmeal
4 T. sugar

Combine ingredients together; place in a plastic zipping bag.
Attach instructions.

Instructions:

Add mix to a large mixing bowl; make a well in the center. In another
bowl, mix 3/4 cup peanut butter and 2 tablespoons honey together;
blend in 2 eggs, beaten, and one cup milk. Pour into well; stir until just
moistened. Fill greased muffin tins half full with batter; place one
teaspoon jelly in center. Add batter until 3/4 full; bake at 375 degrees
for 25 to 30 minutes. Makes 12.

Snuggle up with a steamy cup of hot cocoa after a day of
holiday hustle & bustle. It's a festive (and tasty!) way
to unwind...stir it with a candy cane for a minty touch.

Brownies in a Jar

Cathy Galicia
Pacifica, CA

A sure-fire hit for busy moms!

1 c. all-purpose flour
1/2 t. salt
3/4 c. baking cocoa, divided
1/2 c. brown sugar, packed

1-1/2 c. sugar, divided
1/2 c. chopped nuts
1/2 c. chocolate chips

Combine flour and salt together; spoon into a one-quart, wide-mouth jar. Add 6 tablespoons cocoa; wipe side of jar with paper towel. Layer brown sugar; pack snug. Add layers of 3/4 cup sugar, remaining cocoa and then remaining sugar. Pack down layer of nuts and top with chocolate chips, adding additional chocolate chips if space allows. Secure lid; attach instructions.

Instructions:

Combine brownie mix with 1/2 cup melted butter. Mix in 1/2 teaspoon vanilla extract and 3 beaten eggs; spread mixture in a greased 9"x9" baking pan. Bake at 350 degrees for 35 minutes; cool and cut into squares. Makes 12 servings.

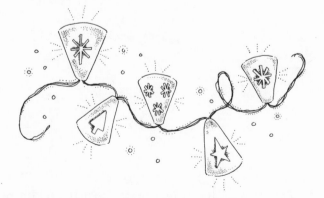

Smells like Christmas! Stir up holiday sentiments by tucking sprigs of balsam & pine between collectibles on a table or mantel.

Christmas Cheer Cookies

Kael Lampe
West Allis, WI

*Whip up a batch and drop off to your friends with some frosting,
jimmies and colored sugars for an afternoon of family fun.*

2-1/2 c. all-purpose flour
1 t. baking soda
1 t. cream of tartar
1-1/2 t. cinnamon
1/2 t. allspice
1/4 t. nutmeg

1/4 t. ground cloves
1 c. butter, softened
1-1/4 c. powdered sugar
1 egg
1 t. vanilla extract
1/2 t. almond extract

Sift dry ingredients together in a bowl; set aside. Cream butter and
sugar in a large mixing bowl; blend in egg and extracts. Add dry
ingredients gradually until well blended; shape dough into a ball. Wrap
dough in plastic wrap; chill for one hour. Roll out dough on a lightly
floured surface to about 1/8-inch thickness; cut into desired shapes
using cookie cutters. Bake on ungreased baking sheets at 350 degrees
for about 8 minutes. Cool on wire racks. Makes about 2 to 3 dozen.

Make a memory with a little one by creating a simple paper
chain...decorate the tree or countdown to the big day with each loop!

Jolly Holidays Jar Cookies

Tonya Sheppard
Galveston, TX

Make 'em, dip 'em and share 'em!

1/4 c. sugar
1/2 c. brown sugar, packed
1-1/2 c. all-purpose flour
3/4 t. baking soda
1/2 t. baking powder
1/2 c. mini green and red
   candy-coated chocolates

1/2 c. quick-cooking oats,
   uncooked
1/2 c. cocoa crispy rice cereal
1/2 c. white chocolate chips

Layer the ingredients in a one-quart, wide-mouth jar in the order
listed; pack down each layer firmly. Tighten the lid; attach
the instructions.

Instructions:

Cream together 1/2 cup butter or margarine, one teaspoon vanilla
extract and one egg in a large mixing bowl; add cookie mix, stirring
until well blended. Drop by teaspoonfuls onto ungreased baking
sheets; bake at 350 degrees for 10 to 12 minutes. Makes about
4 dozen.

Hang up some Christmas
cheer! Tie lengths of
red & green ribbon onto
stained-glass cookies and
hang in a window!

Comet's White Chocolate Crunch
Donna Nowicki
Center City, MN

A favorite of children and reindeer everywhere!

10-oz. pkg. mini pretzels
5 c. doughnut-shaped oat cereal
5 c. bite-size crispy corn
   cereal squares
2 c. peanuts

16-oz. pkg. candy-coated
   chocolates
2 12-oz. pkgs. white chocolate
   chips
3 T. oil

Combine first 5 ingredients in a very large bowl; set aside. Melt chocolate chips with oil in a double boiler; stir until smooth. Pour over cereal mixture; mix well. Spread mixture equally onto 3 wax paper-lined baking sheets; allow to cool. Break into bite-size pieces; store in airtight containers. Makes 5 quarts.

Ice cream cone ornaments add a sweet touch to the tree!
Glue a shiny Christmas tree bulb to the top of an
ice cream cone...just add a hook and it's ready to hang.

Yummy Gifts & Mixes

Santa's Favorite Kettle Corn

Lori Nash
St. Peters, MO

*Serve it warm from the popper or shape into
balls with buttered hands.*

3 T. shortening
1/2 t. vanilla extract
1/2 t. salt

1/2 c. unpopped popcorn
1/2 c. sugar

Melt shortening with vanilla and salt in a 5-quart saucepan; add popcorn. Heat for 30 seconds; sprinkle in sugar. Pop corn over medium-high heat; shake continuously. Remove from heat when popping ends; pour into serving bowl. Makes 3 quarts popped corn.

Whether making Christmas cards or buying them, save a copy
each year and create a scrapbook of greetings. Stir up
sweet memories by looking through the collection
with children and grandchildren.

Chocolate Brittle Surprise

Tami Bowman
Gooseberry Patch

The taste of chocolate-covered toffee can't be beat.
Surprise...it's gone!

35 unsalted saltine crackers	1 c. butter
1 c. brown sugar, packed	2 c. semi-sweet chocolate chips
1 t. vanilla extract	1 c. chopped pecans

Arrange 5 rows of 7 crackers each on a greased, aluminum foil-lined baking sheet; set aside. Add sugar, vanilla and butter to a saucepan; stir over medium heat until dissolved and melted. Pour mixture over crackers; bake at 350 degrees for 17 to 20 minutes. Remove from oven; sprinkle with chocolate chips. Spread chips over the top after melted, about 2 minutes; sprinkle on nuts. Refrigerate one hour; break into pieces. Store in airtight containers. Makes 12 servings.

Deck a tree outside with strings of popcorn and
cranberries...cheery garlands that the birds will love too!

Yummy Gifts & Mixes

Holiday Tiger Spoons

Kelly Alderson
Erie, PA

Try these stirred into your coffee for a sweet treat.

1 c. semi-sweet chocolate chips,
    melted
1 t. butter

24 plastic spoons
3/4 c. white melting chocolate

Melt semi-sweet chocolate chips with butter in a double boiler; dip spoons into melted chocolate. Set aside on wax paper to harden; dip again until desired thickness is achieved. Melt white chocolate in a double boiler; drizzle over dipped spoons. Set aside to harden; wrap individually in plastic wrap. Makes 2 dozen.

Lickety-Split Pecans

Elizabeth Blackstone
Racine, WI

Ready in just 10 minutes and gone before you know it!

1/2 c. sugar
1/4 c. water
1 T. baking cocoa

1/2 t. cinnamon
1/4 t. salt
3 c. pecan halves

Boil all ingredients together for 3 to 5 minutes; stir well to coat pecans. Spread on wax paper to cool; break apart and store in airtight containers. Makes 3 cups.

Get a head start on holiday festivities! Check the local newspapers and church bulletins for once-a-year events like craft bazaars, story-tellings, carolings and the lighting of the tree in Town Square.

Honey-Nut Snack Mix

Jan Ramsey
Wellington, TX

This crunchy sweet snack will remind you of the days when there was a prize in every box!

3/4 c. honey   1 c. salted peanuts
6 c. popped popcorn

Heat honey until thinned and pour over popcorn and peanuts; stir until coated. Spread mixture on an ungreased baking sheet. Bake at 350 degrees until mixture appears dry, about 30 minutes; stir every 5 to 10 minutes. Store in an airtight container. Makes 4 servings.

May you have the gladness of Christmas which is hope;
The spirit of Christmas which is peace;
The heart of Christmas which is love.
- Ada V. Hendricks

Chocolate-Cappuccino Cheesecake
Sandy Stacy
Medway, OH

This makes an absolutely delicious gift...if you can bear to give it away!

1-1/2 c. chopped pecans
1-1/2 c. chocolate wafer cookies, crushed
3/4 c. butter, melted
1/2 c. chocolate chips, melted

Mix pecans, cookies and butter together; press into a greased springform pan. Drizzle with chocolate; chill. Pour filling into crust; bake at 300 degrees for one hour. Reduce heat to 275 degrees and bake for one hour; reduce heat to 250 degrees and bake 30 minutes longer. Cool. Drizzle with topping before serving. Makes 12 servings.

Filling:

16-oz. pkg. cream cheese
1 c. brown sugar, packed
4 eggs
2 t. vanilla extract
1-1/2 c. chocolate chips, melted and cooled
1/3 c. cold coffee
1 c. sour cream

Combine ingredients together; blend until smooth.

Topping:

1/3 c. whipping cream
1 c. sugar
1/2 c. chocolate chips, melted

Stir together until creamy.

Winter Friend Ornament

Jennifer Dutcher
Gooseberry Patch

These are always a hit at our annual Christmas bazaar.

3 mini oval boxes in graduating
  sizes
craft glue
white, black and orange acrylic
  paint
paint brush

12"x1/2" homespun strip
3 mini buttons
toothpick
two small twigs
black ribbon

Glue each box bottom and lid together to prevent each from opening. Paint the large and medium boxes white and the small box black; let dry. Glue the medium box on top of the large box; glue the small box, lid-side down, on top of the medium box. Wrap the homespun around the bottom half of the medium box for a scarf; glue to secure. Glue 3 buttons on the large box; dot 2 round eyes and a mouth on the top half of the medium box. Cut toothpick to desired length for nose; paint orange and glue to the medium box. Glue each twig to the sides of the large box for arms. Loop ribbon and glue on the top of the snowman for hanging.

Clothespin Christmas Tree

Dawn Cochran
Gooseberry Patch

Perfect for teachers' gifts...so easy the kids can help too!

wood stain
old-fashioned wooden
   clothespin
2" dia. fabric circle
jute
mini pine garland

yellow acrylic paint
paint brush
mini wooden star
hot glue
small buttons and bells

Stain clothespin, wipe clean and let dry. Gather homespun around the ball of the clothespin and tie with jute. Cut pine garland in graduated lengths; glue each inside the slot of the clothespin to form a tree shape. Paint star yellow and hot glue to the top of the tree. Hot glue buttons and bells on the ends of the garland for ornaments. Loop jute and hot glue on the back of the tree to hang.

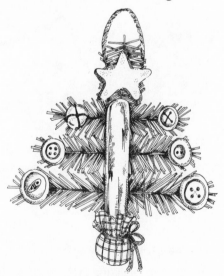

Comb through boxes of vintage ornaments at garage sales, flea markets and antique malls. Pick out handfuls of miniature bulb ornaments to use as one-of-a-kind package tie-ons!

Clip-On Mittens

Janet Pastrick
Gooseberry Patch

Darling on a tree or attached to a bright holiday gift!

scissors
cardboard
felt in holiday colors

glitter
craft glue
wooden clothespins with springs

Cut a mitten shape from the cardboard; use as a pattern to trace mittens onto felt. Cut out mittens and decorate with glitter and scraps of felt using dots, stripes or holiday shapes. Glue a clothespin to the back of each mitten.

Make holiday giftwrap more special and fragrant. Keep a small pail of freshly picked evergreen on your gift-wrapping table...tuck a few sprigs in the ribbon before finishing the bow!

Scented Mug Mats

Brenda Doak
Gooseberry Patch

These smell heavenly when placed under a warm mug.

1/3 yd. holiday fabric
1/4 yd. polyester batting
3 T. whole cloves
3 T. dried orange zest

3 cinnamon sticks,
  finely crushed
jute

Cut twelve, 5-inch squares from fabric and six, 5-inch squares from batting. For each coaster, layer 2 fabric squares, right sides together, and place batting square on top. Machine stitch along all sides, using a 1/4-inch seam allowance; leave a small opening to turn coaster. Trim batting close to stitching, trim corners and turn right-side out. Combine cloves, orange zest and cinnamon pieces; spoon one tablespoon of spice mix into each coaster. Handstitch opening closed on each. Stack coasters and tie together with jute. Makes 6 coasters.

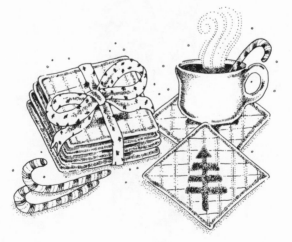

When shipping gifts during the holidays, pack with mess-free materials. Enclose foam peanuts or paper in plastic zipping bags, allowing for easy disposal or reuse.

Candy Topiary

Laura Lett
Gooseberry Patch

Don't we all wish candy grew on trees?

block of floral foam
terra cotta pot
dowel
foam ball

hot glue
wrapped candies
moss
1 yd. ribbon

Cut floral foam to fit in pot; tuck dowel in foam. Secure foam ball on other end of dowel. Using hot glue, completely cover the foam ball with wrapped candies. Cover top of foam block with moss using hot glue. Tie ribbon around the center of the dowel.

For a cheery winter welcome, fill a child's wagon with poinsettias and vintage ornaments and place by the front door.

Christmas Crafts from Gooseberry

Popcorn Stars

Sara Deericks
Gooseberry Patch

Hang these out for the birds too!

wire cutters
16-gauge wire
22-gauge wire

popped popcorn
needle-nose pliers

Use wire cutters to cut three, 12-inch strands of 16-gauge wire. Hold them criss-crossing so that they form a star shape. Wrap 22-gauge wire around them connecting the three wire strands at their centers. Slide popcorn onto each spoke, leaving some space on the end of each wire. Using the pliers, twist the ends of spokes so the popcorn won't fall off. Hang from a tree using the twisted end of one of the spokes.

Add a nostalgic feel to presents by using vintage photographs as gift tags. Photocopy, cut out with decorative-edged scissors and tie onto each package...so easy!

Rooftop Gift Bag

Jenn Bonito
Gooseberry Patch

So sweet filled with fresh-baked goodies.

white paper lunch bag
scissors
colored paper

hole punch
ribbon
craft glue

Fill bag with your gift; fold over top. Cut a rectangle from colored paper for the roof; fold paper over top of bag. Punch two holes through roof and bag; thread ribbon through and tie a bow. Cut decorative shapes from paper and glue on house to embellish with windows, trees, a door and shutters.

Looking for the best way to show off those cherished vintage ornaments? Use floral wire to attach them to a greenery wreath for an easy nostalgic treasure.

Christmas Crafts from Gooseberry

Homespun Garland

Lisa Watkins
Gooseberry Patch

Try using an old-fashioned gingerbread man cutter too!

spray adhesive	scissors
homespun fabric scraps	hole punch
20"x30" white poster board	jute
star cookie cutter	buttons

Use spray adhesive to glue a piece of homespun on each side of the poster board, sandwiching it between the fabric. Using the cookie cutter as a stencil, cut poster board into stars. Punch two holes, side by side, in the center of each star. String jute through holes of stars and buttons; hang from tree or window.

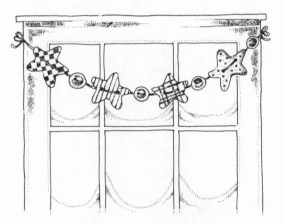

A special thanks for delivering Christmas wishes...add a tin of fudge to your mailbox for the mail carrier!

Flowerpot Christmas Tree

Patti Cooper
Delaware, OH

So welcoming on the front porch or deck.

assorted acrylic paints including
   green and white
paint brush
4 terra cotta pots in graduated
   sizes

sponge, quartered
spray polyurethane

Paint each pot green; let dry. Sponge white paint around the rim of each pot; let dry. Stack pots to form a tree. Use assorted paints to sponge ornaments onto the tree. Spray with polyurethane to seal.

Invite family & friends to share tried & true favorites
and create a holiday recipe scrapbook...a great gift
for a new cook in the family.

Quick & Easy Candles

Tami Bowman
Gooseberry Patch

This is a fun project to make with
a group of friends...set up a crafty assembly line!

decorative-edged scissors
color copies of photos or vintage
   postcards
decorative paper
spray adhesive

purchased jar candles,
   decorative labels removed
gift tags
ribbon

Use scissors to cut out color copies. Cut decorative paper a little larger than the photo to create a mat frame; glue together with spray adhesive. Attach framed photo to the candle jar, using spray adhesive, to create a label. Tie on gift tag with ribbon.

The possibilities for decorating jar candles are endless! Try using
photocopied baby pictures, old-fashioned Christmas seals
or even cut-outs from vintage Christmas cards.

Slim Snowman Ornament

Lora Montgomery
Gooseberry Patch

This little guy looks so cute peeking out of stockings!

cream, black and orange
   acrylic paint
paint brush
large wooden craft stick
hot glue

1-1/2"x1/4" black fabric strip
3-3/4"x3/8" flannel scrap
3 buttons
fine-point black marker
jute

Paint front and back of craft stick with cream paint, leaving 3/4 inch on one end unfinished; let dry. Paint the unfinished end black on both sides; let dry. To form the hat brim, hot glue the black fabric strip to the craft stick where cream and black paint meet. About 3/4 inch below the brim, wrap the flannel strip around the stick and hot glue to secure. Attach the buttons below the scarf using hot glue. Using the wooden handle of the paint brush, dot an orange nose and two black eyes below the hat brim. Using the black marker, complete the snowman face by adding a dotted smile. Loop the jute and hot glue to the back of the snowman's hat for hanging.

For a quick & easy ornament that shimmers, wrap a sparkly pipe cleaner completely around a pencil. Slide it off, bend one end into a hook and hang it on the tree!

Puzzle Piece Snowflake

Roberta Scheeler
Gooseberry Patch

Use beads and sequins to add even more glittery color.

spray paint
8 to 10 small puzzle pieces
craft glue
40 to 50 small metallic beads

spray adhesive
glitter
floral wire

Spray paint front and back of puzzle pieces; let dry. Glue the pieces together, overlapping different sides, forming a snowflake design; glue on beads. Lightly spray adhesive over snowflake; immediately sprinkle on glitter. Use floral wire to attach the snowflake to your tree.

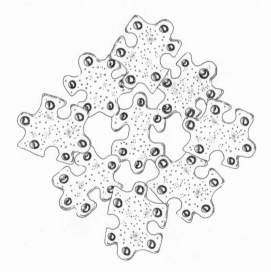

For personalized gift tags, decorate old puzzle pieces
and arrange in the shape of
a friend's initial...so easy!

Memory Tray

Vickie

I made one of these for both Emily and Matt...they love them!

acrylic paint in color of choice
sponge brushes
unfinished wooden serving tray,
   any size
sandpaper or steel wool
ticket stubs, photos, any other
   paper mementos

scissors
matte decoupage medium
paper
craft roller
glass or plexiglass to fit
   inside tray

Paint tray with 2 coats of acrylic paint and let dry 24 hours. Sand paint lightly so that decoupage medium will adhere. Decide how you will arrange pieces, trim any excess and adhere first memento down, using decoupage medium. Put a large, plain piece of paper over the glued image and smooth with roller to eliminate bubbles and ripples. Continue adding images in the same manner and, when all pieces have been pasted, apply a thin coat of decoupage medium to the entire tray, covering all pasted surfaces. Let dry for about 30 minutes. Apply 2 or 3 additional coats of the medium to seal, allowing 30 minutes to dry between each coat. After the final layer is dry, set the glass or plexiglass on top to protect the tray.

Mosaic Herb Garden

Jo Ann

*Garden gifts are great any time of year...you'll be surprised
how quick & easy this really is!*

hot glue
broken ceramic tiles
4 3" dia. terra cotta pots
grout
spoon

sponge, moistened
potting soil
4 plastic zipping bags
herb seed packets
Optional: 12" long wooden crate

Glue ceramic pieces to the pots in desired pattern, leaving room
between for grout; allow to dry for at least 8 hours. Mix up grout
powder according to package directions and spoon grout onto the side
of each pot. Smooth into spaces between ceramic tiles with the back
of a spoon. Use a wet sponge to remove the excess from the surface
of the tiles. Let pots sit for at least 12 hours. Spoon potting soil into
4 small plastic zipping bags, add seed packets and place inside each
pot. Place filled pots inside crate, if desired.

Mosaic terra cotta pots make great gifts in a set or on their own.
Fill them with craft supplies or pens and pencils and make a handy
organizer or just dress up a favorite potted plant!

Berry Beaded Wreath

Jen Licon-Conner
Gooseberry Patch

Add a handful of gold beads for extra sparkle.

red nail polish
flat-head straight pins
red seam binding
8-inch foam wreath form

red beads, varying sizes
craft glue
red satin ribbon

Using the nail polish, paint the heads of the straight pins red; let dry. Pin one end of the seam binding to the wreath form, and wrap it around the entire form, overlapping it slightly to completely cover the form. Cut the end of the binding and secure to form with a pin. Slide a bead onto a pin, dip in craft glue and push the pin into form. Pin the larger beads onto the wreath first, then fill in any holes with the smaller beads. Continue pinning beads until the front and side of the form are covered completely. Loop the ribbon and secure with glue to hang.

Fool the package-shakers in the family by disguising smaller gifts in oversized boxes...they'll never guess!

'Twas the Night Before Christmas

The night before...it's almost here,
gather 'round for Christmas cheer!

Nancy Hauer
Rifle, CO

I grew up on a beautiful cattle ranch in the mountains of western Colorado. Our place was nestled snugly into the "V" formed by two mountains. It was a wonderful place year 'round, with acres and acres for a young girl to explore...but at Christmastime it became even more magical. I loved going out in mid-December to cut our tree and, each year, I anxiously wondered what spot Dad would choose to find one. We would usually drive the pickup or the old Jeep, but one year, when I was 8 or 9 years old, Dad said we could go on horseback! I remember the wonder of it all, my dad in the lead on Stormy, my brother in the middle and me bringing up the rear. We headed off to the southeast of the house across a rocky hillside in search of the perfect tree. As our horses climbed, we got into deeper snow and gradually entered into true Christmas tree country. We dismounted to continue our search on foot, and together the three of us selected a beautiful, tall, cone-shaped tree. But we weren't finished yet...we also had to find Mom's tree, the smaller one she always had on the buffet table in the dining room which was decorated with her special ornaments. We also cut one for my grandmother who lived in town and then it was time to return home. Oh, if I only had pictures! There we were, Dad pulling our big, beautiful tree behind him, my brother carrying Mom's special tree and me in the back carrying Grandmother's. Even the horses and dogs seemed to sense our excitement as we rode toward home singing Christmas songs in our merriest voices.

Merry Memories

Terry Zaccuri
Costa Mesa, CA

One of my favorite holiday traditions is spending an afternoon with my sisters decorating gingerbread cookies. I bake the cookies the day before we get together. The next morning, I make powdered sugar frosting and separate it into three bowls, tinting one red, one green and leaving one white. When the girls arrive, we put the frosting into pastry bags and we're ready to have some fun! We spend an afternoon together decorating the cookies, drinking hot apple cider and listening to Christmas music. It's a time to ourselves when we can talk and laugh. We sample some of the cookies too! Everyone gets cookies to take home where we each display them on our own fireplace mantels. They look so cute for the holidays and smell great!

Sandra Lee Smith
Arleta, CA

One year, just before Christmas, I brought home little artificial trees and a bunch of small ornaments to decorate them with. I couldn't resist inviting some of my co-workers' children to join us in decorating and, when we all gathered, we ended up with a group of 11! I also had a large tree cookie cutter and made up a batch of sugar cookies and green frosting. We had all kinds of decorations for the cookies...red cinnamon candies, silver balls, tiny chocolate-coated candy and chocolate chips. After the children had decorated their artificial tree, which of course they got to take home, they decorated the cookies. Some immediately ate their cookies and others took them home to share. The following year, I hosted another gathering and I had to make lots of extra cookies because all the moms wanted to decorate them too!

Tammy Buller
Douglas, OK

One of my favorite Christmas traditions from my childhood is when, a week before Christmas, my mother would put on Christmas music, turn on the lights of all the decorations in our house and put out snacks, cookies and drinks. Then my father, mother, sister and I would get ready to wrap presents together. My father did the wrapping, my sister tied the bows and my mother labeled the packages. I was the youngest so I did the running and retrieving of presents from the closet to the table and then delivered them under the tree. It always encouraged me that it is just as good to give as well as to receive. Those fond family memories will always be with me as I think of how much fun it is to get ready for Christmas.

Carol Brashear
Myerstown, PA

When I was growing up, my grandmother always gave us flannel pajamas for Christmas. Now that I have a family of my own, I always make sure my children have new flannel pajamas or nightgowns to wear Christmas Eve. I have even made them each a pair and flannel pants for my husband. It is the one gift they get to open on Christmas Eve. The pajamas always remind me of my grandmother.

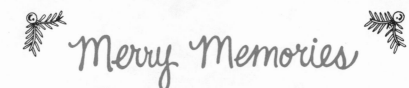

Merry Memories

Joanne Quinn
San Francisco, CA

When I was a child, on the Sunday before Christmas, my grandparents would take me to the Italian-American Social Club Christmas party. It was such a special treat. There was always a magician to amaze us and a local dance studio would entertain as well. Of course, the highlight of the afternoon was the arrival of Santa with his bag of presents. He always seemed to have exactly the perfect gift for me. Once all the gifts were distributed, hot dogs, chips and ice cream were served. As if all that wasn't enough to make a perfect day, when I returned home, our tree was completely lit and decorated…courtesy of Santa's elves, Mom & Dad. Many years later, when my children were young, my parents continued the tradition by taking them to the Christmas party. It was something that they looked forward to every year and it brought back many happy memories for me!

Shawna Searle
Burley, ID

I remember Mother telling me a Christmas story of her youth. One year, Grandma & Grandpa couldn't afford traditional wrapping paper, so Santa wrapped his packages that year in brown butcher paper. (I find this interesting because, today, many people decorate their gifts this way on purpose to achieve a simple, country look.) Mother had awakened in the night and toddled into Grandma & Grandpa's room. She announced with tear-stained cheeks that Santa had only brought packages of meat this year! What a relief it was when, after a few laughs, she found out otherwise.

Angela Stacy
Hilliard, OH

Each year my family, as well as my three sisters and their families, travel to my parents' home for a Christmas celebration. When Grandpa disappears, we begin to share Christmas stories and sing festive songs, while the children listen for the ringing of the bell that announces that Santa has arrived. When Santa enters, one can hear the squeals of excitement and see the awe in our children's eyes. When the children are individually placed on Santa's lap, not only do my sisters and I see the magic reflected as they look up at Santa, but we also see that same magic in the eyes of their grandfather gazing down at them.

Patricia Husek
St. Joseph, MI

Ever since our children were young, my husband has loved playing Santa. He'd buy lots of small candies & treats and wrap each of them individually. He wanted our kids to have lots of gifts to open but also because they loved all those gifts "From Santa." When all the gifts had been opened, he'd always say that he was getting a mysterious "headache." He'd say that it came from not being able to remember something. We'd all walk around the house with him trying to help him "remember." Eventually, he'd lead us to where something the whole family had wished for, the biggest present of all, was hidden. Of course, every year, the tag read "From Santa."

Merry Memories

Robin Kile
Franklin, WV

I have been teaching reading to elementary-aged students for the last 16 years and, for each of those many years, I've been making Christmas ornaments for my students, fellow teachers and family members. I make and give about 100 ornaments each year! My yearly tradition begins in the Fall and by Christmas, there are many different kinds of ornaments made. I hang them on my classroom tree a couple of weeks before Christmas. During this time, students admire the different ones, deciding which ones they admire most. A day or so before Christmas vacation, we "un-decorate" the classroom tree...each student choosing the ornament he or she has had their eye on. It is a delight to hear their comments and watch as they are given the opportunity to choose their favorites.

Gerry Werner
Centereach, NY

Starting December 1st, my family plans a Christmas activity for each day of the month. We write out everything we want to do and choose a day for each. Some things are simple like watching a fun holiday video or making stamped wrapping paper. Other things might include making birdfeeders, touring the neighborhood to look at light displays or attending a school concert. We try to do something every day...occasionally, we may miss one, but overall, the month is filled with fun holiday spirit!

Karina Solomon
Inkom, ID

Every Christmas Eve, my sisters, brother and I would all sleep in the same room...usually my parents'. Mom & Dad would wake early and creep downstairs. We'd ring a bell to let them know we were awake and they'd meet us in the hallway, line us up, youngest to oldest. Then we'd all scramble out to the tree to see what Santa had brought us. Once gifts from Santa had been opened and played with, we'd sit down in a big circle and open up the rest of our gifts.

Wendy Lee Paffenroth
Pine Island, NY

Our Christmas stockings always held little items that our children could use. They always got a new toothbrush, some little samples of lotions and we never forgot to put in a package of blank thank-you cards. They always got the hint. Now that my children are teenagers, their stockings contain other things like fishing bobbers or a new lipstick...of course, they still get the thank-you cards!

Merry Memories

Pat Emery
Denison, TX

When I was a child, I was notorious for shaking my packages and carefully unwrapping them and wrapping them back up so I could find out what was inside! One particular year, my mom, in her sneaky wisdom, decided she would fix me. There was a long box about the size of a doll box under the tree. True to my curious self, I shook it. There was something in it that rolled form one end to the other; it was heavy and large. I did everything but unwrap the gift to try to figure out what was in it. Every night, I would take the opportunity to check out that package, but to no success. Then on Christmas morning, I was allowed to unwrap the gift. What was it? A coconut, loose in that big doll box, was all that was rolling back and forth! Mom and Santa won that year. Mom has passed away, but I will always remember that coconut with fond memories.

Dottie Freeland
Cedar Falls, IA

The Christmas that my father was on strike will always be one of my favorites. We had very little money and toys for my 2 sisters and me were a luxury we really couldn't afford. Even so, my father went to the drugstore just before they closed on Christmas Eve. There were three dolls left on the shelf, all the same except for the colors of their dresses. He bought them for a dollar each and put them under the tree for us. We were so excited that each of us got our own toy and a beautiful doll at that. Even though there wasn't a string to pull and she didn't talk, in my imagination, she could do anything!

Carol Burns
Gooseberry Patch

A few years ago, our youngest daughter who was 3 years old, the age when they insist they can "do" everything themselves, decided she would dress herself for Christmas Eve Service as a present to us. At the time we figured "what a relief" because we had already ironed and laid out her clothes and were busy preparing dinner and such for later on that evening. It was time to leave and our other 3 children plus the two of us were ready when, there she came...clomp, clomp, clomping down the stairs. She had on her beautiful new Christmas dress, but wait, those were not her brand new patent leather shoes. She was wearing her favorite bright yellow rubber boots that she had unearthed from somewhere deep in the depths of her closet! So proud, she stood there twirling in the mirror, "I dressed myself and I look beautiful!" With 4 pairs of expectant eyes staring at me, what could a mom say, other than agree that she was indeed just as beautiful as could be. At church that evening, the little Cherub Choir all danced down the aisle...all except one who clomped, clomped, clomped just a little bit prouder than the rest.

Merry Memories

Kay Bennecoff
Shoemakersville, PA

Christmas of 1984 wasn't looking like it was going to be any fun at all...it certainly didn't start out well, that's for sure. My father had been diagnosed with cancer and would be spending the holidays in the hospital. He absolutely adores his family (and Christmas) and we couldn't imagine not being together. Even though my 18-month-old little girl, Jaime was anticipating Christmas with such glee you couldn't help but delight in her joy, her big brother, Jason was very worried about his PopPop being in the hospital for Christmas. On top of everything, I didn't know if my dad was going to be here for next Christmas. With all this in mind, I decided to go all out and make this "the best Christmas ever." I bought the most beautiful dress for Jaime and she looked absolutely angelic. My husband went to the hospital and was able to bring my dad home on Christmas Eve Day. We got him all dressed up and drove him to our house. He was able to enjoy his whole family together in one big room on Christmas Eve. As tears ran down his face and ours, I knew that we'd done the right thing. I'm very happy to say that since then, we continue to celebrate year after year with Dad but we'll never forget that year...it's still the best ever.

Linda Murdock
Selah, WA

One thing our children did during the holidays was to pray for snow and hope to have it actually happen...overnight! They were so excited when it snowed because that meant their dad would hook up the sled to the family pick-up and pull them around in the field. One, two and sometimes three would be on that sled. One child would be up in front of the pick-up with dad, one on the sidelines with the movie camera, and the others sitting in the back of the pick-up with the back open so they could dangle their legs...all of them laughing and having a good time. I watched from the kitchen and listened and enjoyed their laughter while getting ready for their return with hot cocoa and marshmallows waiting.

They're older now, some with little ones of their own and no matter their ages, they still get excited for snow! This last Christmas, as soon as the snow arrived, I heard "Hey dad, how about getting out the sleds and heading to the field with the pick-up?" And away they would go. Only this time, they took turns driving some of their own children. I watched and laughed and felt joy in seeing my family have a good time, while tending to babes too small to take part, knowing that their turn would also come soon enough.

Merry Memories

Katherine Henry
Moncton, New Brunswick

I remember my mother at Christmastime getting ready for the village craft fair. She would be knitting a sweater or slippers or crocheting an afghan. Our cat, Midnight, would be playing in Mom's balls of yarn and tangling herself into a mess that I would have to untangle later. My sister and brother would be fighting over another game of Monopoly...my brother always cheated. I would sit on my mother's feet and keep them warm while I watched my favorite Christmas movies. I sipped Mom's homemade cocoa, dreaming of what old St. Nick might bring me this year.

Denise Rounds
Tulsa, OK

Before the rush of Christmas shopping and baking gets under way, I invite friends I haven't seen recently to a Christmas tea for two with me. I call them ahead to coordinate our calendars and ask for just an hour of their time. I follow that with a personally written invitation in the mail. I enjoy planning ahead what baked goods I will prepare for these teas and often bake several things that I know freeze well to give me ease prior to each tea. It is relaxing and easy entertaining as the house is already decorated for Christmas. Candles are lit, carols are played, hot Christmas tea is poured and sweet conversations begin. It doesn't take much time to catch up and refresh ourselves. This is one of my very favorite means of touching base with the friends I've made over the years and it gives them a Christmas gift of refreshment.

Sausage & Apple Appetizers

Kathy Grashoff
Fort Wayne, IN

Try doubling this recipe...they always go fast!

2 T. butter
1 onion, chopped
1/2 c. apple jelly
1/2 c. brown sugar, packed
2-lb. pkg. smoked cocktail
    wieners

3 apples, cored, peeled and
    sliced
2 T. water
1 T. cornstarch

Melt butter in a 10" skillet over medium-high heat; sauté onion until golden. Stir in jelly and brown sugar until dissolved; add wieners. Reduce heat to medium-low; cook for 20 minutes or until mixture thickens, stirring occasionally. Add apples; cover and heat 10 minutes more or until apples are tender. Combine water and cornstarch in a small bowl; stir into apple mixture. Heat until thickened, 2 to 3 minutes; remove from heat and serve warm. Makes about 30 servings.

For a whimsical holiday decoration, make a wreath of sparkly gumdrops or Christmas peppermints! Secure gumdrops with toothpicks in a wreath form or glue on wrapped candies.

Snacks to Nibble

Yuletide Wassail

Kristine Marumoto
Sandy, UT

Warm up with a cup after a day of playing in the snow!

2 c. sugar
6-1/2 c. water, divided
1/4 t. allspice
1/8 t. ground cloves
1/8 t. ground ginger

12-oz. can frozen orange juice
    concentrate
6-oz. can frozen lemonade
    concentrate
2 qts. apple cider

Combine sugar and 4 cups water in a 5-quart saucepan; boil for
5 minutes. Add remaining ingredients; heat thoroughly before
serving. Makes 18 to 24 servings.

Pumpkin Dip

Jennifer Leonard
Maumee, OH

Serve with gingersnaps, vanilla wafers or graham crackers
for a sweet treat.

1-lb. pkg. powdered sugar
2 8-oz. pkgs. cream cheese,
    softened

30-oz. can pumpkin pie filling
2 t. cinnamon
1 t. ground ginger

Blend powdered sugar and cream cheese together until fluffy; mix
in pumpkin pie filling, cinnamon and ginger. Cover and chill. Makes
7 cups.

Parmesan Spread

Melissa Weston
Scotia, NY

A family favorite! Serve with hearty crackers...don't forget the holiday spreaders.

8-oz. pkg. cream cheese, softened
1/3 c. grated Parmesan cheese

1/4 c. mayonnaise
1 t. dried oregano
1/4 t. garlic powder

Blend ingredients together in a medium-size mixing bowl; cover and chill for at least one hour before serving. Makes about 1-1/2 cups.

Cheese Buttons

Gena Pederson
Minot, ND

Named for their cute-as-a-button size!

6 eggs
2-1/2 c. all-purpose flour
1 c. cottage cheese

1/2 t. salt
water
butter for frying

Mix eggs, flour, cottage cheese and salt together; drop by teaspoonfuls into a stockpot of boiling water. Boil for 10 minutes; drain. Fry in butter until light golden. Serves 6.

Serve holiday snacks & treats on a peppermint stick tray! Cut
a piece of cardboard into the desired tray size and
cover with peppermint sticks using royal icing
as "glue"...allow to harden overnight.

Tomato-Cheese Ball

Judy Cheatham
Brentwood, TN

Serve with crunchy bread rounds on a bed of crispy lettuce...yum!

1 c. canned tomatoes, drained
   and chopped
8-oz. pkg. cream cheese,
   softened
2 c. shredded Cheddar cheese
1/2 c. margarine, softened

1/2 c. onion, chopped
1/4 t. garlic powder
1 t. salt
1/4 t. red pepper flakes
1 c. chopped pecans

Combine first 8 ingredients, blending well. Place in a bowl and freeze for one hour. Mold into a ball; roll in pecans. Freeze for one more hour. Before serving, bring to room temperature. Serves 8.

Surprise a neighbor with gifts at the doorstep! Make a paper cone from vintage giftwrap and hang it from their doorknob...fill with candy canes and sweet treats.

Zucchini Appetizers

Melissa Berlin
Titusville, PA

*Arrange on a platter with cherry tomatoes and yellow
bell peppers for a splash of holiday color.*

3 c. zucchini, peeled and diced
1 c. buttermilk biscuit
    baking mix
4 eggs, beaten
1/2 c. onion, chopped

1/2 c. grated Parmesan cheese
2 T. dried parsley
1/2 t. salt
1 clove garlic, minced
1/2 c. oil

Mix all the ingredients together; spread into a greased 13"x9" baking
dish. Bake at 350 degrees for 25 minutes; cut into squares and serve
warm. Makes 2 dozen.

Revive a childhood
tradition...add an
old-fashioned toy train
(complete with a whistle!)
under the tree this year.

For Sale
TREES

Snacks to Nibble

Crab Dip

Susan Biffignani
Fenton, MO

Passed on to me from a friend at school, this dip's so simple!

2 8-oz. pkgs. cream cheese,
   softened
1 c. sour cream
1.4-oz. pkg. dry vegetable
   soup mix

12-oz. bottle cocktail sauce
6-oz. can crabmeat, drained

Blend cream cheese until fluffy; mix in sour cream and soup mix. Mound on a small serving platter; pour cocktail sauce on top. Sprinkle with crabmeat; cover and chill for at least one hour before serving. Makes about 3 cups.

Come & Get 'Em Meatballs

Tori Current
Veedersburg, IN

*Easy to put in the oven before we leave the
house...when we return, they're ready!*

2 lbs. ground beef
1-1/2 oz. pkg. dry onion soup
   mix
1 c. bread crumbs
3 eggs, beaten
1 T. dry mustard

16-oz. can cranberry sauce
12-oz. bottle chili sauce
14-oz. can sauerkraut, drained
   and rinsed
1-1/2 c. water
2/3 c. brown sugar, packed

Mix first 5 ingredients together; shape into walnut-size balls. Arrange in an ungreased 13"x9" baking pan; set aside. Combine remaining ingredients in a saucepan; simmer for 10 minutes. Pour over meatballs; cover tightly with aluminum foil. Bake at 350 degrees for 2 hours. Serves 6.

Roasted Red Pepper Salsa

Shawna Lloyd
Flint, TX

Fry up some quartered corn tortillas for your own fresh chips.

2 c. corn
2 tomatoes, diced
7-oz. jar roasted red peppers,
    drained and chopped
2 green onions, finely chopped
1 jalapeño pepper, seeded
    and minced
3 T. fresh cilantro, minced

2 T. lime juice
1 T. white vinegar
1/2 t. salt
1/4 t. pepper
1/4 t. cumin
2 avocados, peeled, pitted
    and chopped

Gently stir all the ingredients together; cover and refrigerate at least
2 hours before serving. Makes 2-1/2 cups.

Welcome guests for the holidays! Tie plump velvet bows on potted
evergreens and place on either side of the front door.

Fiesta Nachos

Mary Bettuchy
Duxbury, MA

Company coming? Better make a double batch!

15-oz. bag tortilla chips
1 lb. ground beef, browned
1-1/2 c. shredded Cheddar
  cheese
1-1/2 c. shredded Monterey
  Jack cheese

2 c. sour cream
2 c. salsa
1 sweet onion, diced
1 bunch green onions, chopped
2 tomatoes, diced
Optional: sliced black olives

Layer tortilla chips over the bottom of a 13"x9" baking pan; top with ground beef. Sprinkle with Cheddar and Monterey Jack cheeses. Bake at 375 degrees for 10 to 15 minutes, or until cheese is melted. Remove from oven; layer with sour cream and then salsa. Top with onions and tomatoes; add olives, if desired. Makes 12 servings.

Headed to a Christmas Eve gathering? Take along a fresh-baked coffee cake for the hostess...a thoughtful timesaver she'll appreciate Christmas morning!

Bacon-Cheese Toast

Tina Knotts
Gooseberry Patch

Just right for munching!

1-lb. pkg. bacon, crisply cooked
  and crumbled
3 c. shredded provolone cheese

1/2 c. mayonnaise
2-1/2 T. onion, minced
1 loaf sliced white cocktail bread

Combine first 4 ingredients; spread on bread slices. Place on an ungreased baking sheet; bake at 325 degrees for 13 to 15 minutes or until golden. Serves 8 to 10.

Water Chestnut Roll-Ups

Sue Thomas
Butler, OH

My three sisters and I especially enjoy these around the holidays but they're great anytime!

2 lbs. bacon, sliced in half
3 8-oz. cans whole
  water chestnuts

2 c. brown sugar, packed
2 c. catsup

Roll one strip bacon around each water chestnut; secure with a toothpick. Arrange on a baking sheet; bake at 350 degrees for 30 minutes or until bacon is browned. Combine remaining ingredients together; pour half in the bottom of a 3 to 4-quart slow cooker. Place water chestnuts in slow cooker; pour remaining sauce on top. Cook on low for 1-1/2 hours. Serves 12 to 15.

Snacks to Nibble

Broccoli-Cheese Dip

Valerie Blazer
Millersburg, OH

Serve with crackers, bread sticks or alongside fresh veggies.

10-oz. pkg. frozen broccoli cuts
10-3/4 oz. can cream of
   mushroom soup
1/2 c. shredded sharp Cheddar
   cheese

1/4 c. mayonnaise
1 egg, beaten
1/4 c. milk
1/4 c. bread crumbs
1 T. butter, melted

Steam broccoli until crisp-tender; drain in a colander for 10 minutes. Spread in a 8"x8" baking dish; set aside. Stir soup, cheese, mayonnaise and egg together; gradually mix in milk. Pour over broccoli; set aside. Combine bread crumbs and butter in a small bowl; sprinkle over broccoli. Bake at 350 degrees for 45 minutes. Makes about 4 cups.

Set the mood at
holiday parties
with jolly Christmas music!
Invite guests to bring their
favorites and have a festive
variety all evening long!

Cheery Cheese Ring

Wendy Lee Paffenroth
Pine Island, NY

*The sweetness in the preserves tames the tangy bite in
the cheese...a perfect complement served on crispy crackers.*

16 oz. sharp Cheddar cheese,
   finely grated
4 oz. cream cheese, softened
1/4 c. mayonnaise
1 onion, minced

1 c. chopped walnuts
1/4 t. garlic powder
1/8 t. chili powder
1/8 t. hot pepper sauce
1 c. strawberry preserves

Combine all ingredients except the strawberry preserves in a large
mixing bowl; blend well. Scoop the mixture onto a serving platter; wet
your hands and shape into a ring. Pour strawberry preserves into the
center. Serves 12.

Raspberry Cider

Sue Osburn
Hot Springs, AR

Snuggle in with a cup of this fruity cider.

1 qt. apple cider
12-oz. jar raspberry jelly
1 t. sweetened lemonade
   drink mix

1/8 t. unsweetened raspberry-
   flavored drink mix
Garnish: lemon slices

Bring cider to a boil in a 3-quart saucepan; add remaining ingredients.
Stir until jelly dissolves; remove from heat. Pour into serving mugs
while still warm; garnish with a lemon slice. Serves 4.

Bring the sounds of the season to the table...thread jingle bells onto
thin wire and twist into a napkin holder.

Raspberry-Cheese Spread

Pamela Carroll
Weimar, TX

*Shape into a holiday star or even a candy cane
for an eye-catching appetizer.*

8-oz. pkg. pasteurized process
   cheese spread, grated
16 oz. Cheddar cheese, grated
4 green onions, chopped

1/2 c. chopped pecans
1/3 c. mayonnaise-type salad
   dressing
raspberry jam

Combine all ingredients together except for the jam. Press into desired
shape or a plastic wrap-lined mold; chill until firm. Remove from mold
and spread with jam. Serves 8 to 10.

Look for vintage cake molds in festive shapes at flea markets and
antique shops. Use these old-fashioned molds to shape
this spread for an extra-special treat!

Brown Sugar Pecans

Nancy Wise
Little Rock, AR

*Seems I am forever making these throughout the holiday season.
My family eats them before they're even cooled!*

16-oz. pkg. pecan halves
1/2 c. butter
3/4 c. brown sugar, packed

2 t. vanilla extract
1/4 t. salt

Arrange pecan halves in an aluminum foil-lined 13"x9" baking pan;
set aside. Melt butter in a saucepan over medium heat; add sugar,
vanilla and salt. Stir one minute; remove from heat. Continue stirring
until sugar dissolves; pour over pecans, stirring to coat. Bake at
325 degrees for 25 to 35 minutes; stir every 10 to 15 minutes.
Remove from oven; spread on wax paper to
cool. Store in an airtight container. Makes
12 servings.

Stir up some memories...invite
Grandma & Grandpa to read
Christmas stories to little ones
and share holiday stories from
their childhood.

Sweets for Santa

Party Pralines

Lora Cheney
Cedar Park, TX

Last-minute guests? These'll wow them!

1 c. sugar
1/2 c. brown sugar, packed
1/4 c. milk

1 T. butter
1 c. chopped pecans
1 t. vanilla extract

Combine first 5 ingredients in a saucepan; boil for 1-1/2 minutes.
Remove from heat; stir in vanilla. Blend until creamy; drop by
teaspoonfuls onto wax paper. Cool; store in an airtight container.
Makes about 24.

Chocolate Comfort

Emily Johnson
Lyons, IN

What could be better than rich, homemade chocolate pudding?

1 c. sugar
1/4 c. cornstarch
1/2 c. baking cocoa
1/2 t. salt

4 c. milk
2 T. butter
2 t. vanilla extract

Combine dry ingredients in a heavy 2-quart saucepan; heat over
medium heat. Gradually add milk; stir constantly. Boil for 2 minutes.
Remove from heat; stir in butter and vanilla. Serve warm or chilled.
Serves 6.

Chocolate-Orange Balls

Cindy Thompson
San Diego, CA

*These taste best when made early in December
and stored for a week or two.*

6-oz. pkg. semi-sweet chocolate
   chips
1/2 c. sugar
3 T. corn syrup
1/2 c. orange juice

2-1/2 c. vanilla wafers, crushed
1 c. chopped nuts
Garnish: assortment of colored
   sugars

Combine chocolate chips, sugar and corn syrup in a heavy saucepan; heat and stir until chocolate is melted. Remove from heat; stir in orange juice. Add vanilla wafer crumbs and nuts; mix well. Chill until firm. Form dough into one-inch balls; roll in colored sugar. Store in an airtight container for up to 3 to 4 weeks. Makes about one pound.

To keep freshly baked cookies from sticking together, make sure they're completely cooled before packing...they'll go easily from storage to serving tray.

Sweets for Santa

Grandma's Best Sugar Cookies

Grace Yanke
Howard City, MI

My mother gave me this recipe 51 years ago when I married. I can still remember her baking these on her wood-burning range before electric was around. Now my grandchildren help with the baking and decorating. It's such a comfort to know that the tradition continues.

2/3 c. shortening
1-1/3 c. sugar, divided
2 eggs, beaten
1/2 t. vanilla extract
3 c. all-purpose flour

2 t. baking powder
1/2 t. salt
1/3 c. milk
Optional: colored powdered
   sugar frosting

Cream shortening in a large mixing bowl; gradually blend in one cup sugar. Mix in eggs and vanilla; set aside. Combine flour, baking powder and salt together; blend into sugar mixture alternately with milk. Roll dough out on a lightly floured surface; cut into desired shapes using cookie cutters. Sprinkle with remaining sugar; bake on ungreased baking sheets at 350 degrees for 10 to 12 minutes. Cool on wire racks; frost with colored frosting, if desired. Makes 4 dozen.

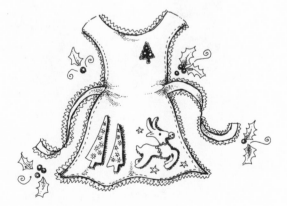

Pineapple Cookies

Debbie Driggers
Greenville, TX

*Pineapples are a sign of hospitality...baking them into
these cookies says, "Welcome one and all!"*

2/3 c. shortening
1-1/4 c. sugar
1 t. vanilla extract
1 egg
2 c. all-purpose flour
2 t. baking powder

1/2 t. salt
3/4 c. crushed pineapple,
   drained
1/2 c. flaked coconut
1/2 c. chopped pecans

Cream shortening, sugar and vanilla together; blend in egg. Mix in
flour, baking powder, salt and pineapple; gently stir in coconut and
pecans. Drop by teaspoonfuls onto ungreased baking sheets; bake
at 325 degrees until golden, about 10 to 12 minutes. Makes about
3 dozen.

Festive CD storage for all those Christmas favorites...decoupage
vintage-style gift wrap to the sides of a small wooden crate. So easy!

Lyda's Gingerbread Cookies

Eula Preston
Zanesville, OH

This recipe has been used for 4 generations...Lyda, my mother, gave it to me and I've shared it with my children & grandchildren as well!

1 c. shortening
1 c. brown sugar, packed
3/4 c. molasses
3/4 c. buttermilk
2 eggs

4-1/2 c. all-purpose flour
3 t. ground ginger
2 t. baking soda
1 t. salt
sugar

Cream shortening and brown sugar together; add molasses, buttermilk and eggs. Blend well; set aside. In a separate mixing bowl, sift flour, ginger, baking soda and salt together; combine into buttermilk mixture. Mix well; cover and refrigerate overnight. Roll out dough on a lightly floured surface to 1/4-inch thickness; cut into desired shapes using cookie cutters. Sprinkle with sugar; bake at 400 degrees for 10 to 12 minutes. Makes about 5 dozen.

Hand deliver edible Christmas cards this year. Just cut gingerbread into postcard-size pieces, bake and pipe on holiday wishes with royal icing...top off with gumdrops and candy canes!

Snowballs

Jill Duvendack
Pioneer, OH

*I make these delicious cookies during the first snow every year but,
since everyone loves them so much, I end up making a triple batch!*

3/4 c. butter, softened
1/2 c. sugar
1 egg
2 t. vanilla extract

2 c. all-purpose flour
1 c. chopped pecans
1 c. chocolate chips
powdered sugar

Cream butter and sugar together; stir in egg and vanilla. Blend in
flour; fold in pecans and chocolate chips. Form into walnut-size balls;
place on ungreased baking sheets. Bake at 350 degrees for 15 to
20 minutes; cool. Roll in powdered sugar several times to coat well;
store in an airtight container. Makes 3 to 3-1/2 dozen.

Christmas Crunch

Charlotte Wolfe
Ft. Lauderdale, FL

*Drizzle with melted white chocolate and sprinkle
with coconut for a "snowy" treat.*

1 c. sugar
1 c. corn syrup

1 c. crunchy peanut butter
10 c. corn flake cereal

Combine sugar and corn syrup in a heavy 2-quart saucepan; boil until
sugar dissolves. Remove from heat; stir in peanut butter until melted.
Pour over corn flakes in a large mixing bowl; stir to coat as evenly as
possible. Spread and press onto a buttered baking sheet; cut into
squares while still warm. Makes about 2-1/2 dozen.

French Cream Cookies

Jennifer Vallimont
Spruce Creek, PA

Heavenly dunked in rich & creamy cocoa.

2 c. all-purpose flour
1 t. baking soda
1 t. cream of tartar
1/4 t. salt
1/2 c. butter
1/2 c. shortening

1/2 c. creamy peanut butter
1-1/2 c. powdered sugar
1 egg, beaten
1 t. vanilla extract
sugar

Sift first 4 ingredients together; set aside. Cream butter, shortening and peanut butter together in a large mixing bowl until fluffy; add powdered sugar, mixing well. Blend in egg and vanilla; mix in dry ingredients. Cover dough; refrigerate until firm. Shape dough into walnut-size balls; place on ungreased baking sheets. Flatten slightly with the bottom of a glass dipped in sugar; bake at 350 degrees for 12 minutes. Cool on baking sheets for 2 minutes; remove to wire rack to cool completely. Makes about 3 dozen.

Spread Christmas cheer during holiday travels. Tie a festive evergreen wreath to the grill of the family car...don't forget the bow!

Molasses Sugar Cookies

Jo Ann Cross
Blue Springs, MO

Even better the next day!

3/4 c. shortening
1 c. sugar
1/4 c. molasses
1 egg
2 t. baking soda
2 c. all-purpose flour

1 t. ground cloves
2 t. cinnamon
1 t. ground ginger
1/2 t. salt
additional sugar for coating

Cream shortening, sugar and molasses together; mix in remaining ingredients except for additional sugar. Roll dough into walnut-size balls; coat with additional sugar. Place on greased baking sheets; bake at 375 degrees for 10 minutes. Makes 3 to 4 dozen.

Stencil a snowflake design on an old-fashioned
lunch tin...fill with cookies and goodies for a quick holiday gift.

✺ Sweets for Santa ◉

Nan's Shortbread Cookies

Mary-Lynn Reilly
Lutz, FL

For a lemon version, just add one teaspoon vanilla, 2 tablespoons lemon zest and 2 tablespoons poppy seed to the recipe.

1 c. butter
1/2 c. sugar

2 c. all-purpose flour

Cream butter and sugar together; add flour, mixing well. Pat into a 1/4-inch thick rectangle; cut out desired shapes using floured cookie cutters. Arrange on ungreased baking sheets; prick tops lightly with a fork. Bake at 300 degrees for 25 to 30 minutes. Makes about 2 dozen.

Montana Winter Spiced Cider

Linda Reynolds
Cut Bank, MT

It gets cold here in Montana...not just anything will warm you like this hug in a mug!

3/4 c. brown sugar, packed
1 t. cinnamon
1/2 c. vanilla ice cream, softened

2 T. butter, softened
1-1/2 gal. apple cider

Combine the first 4 ingredients together in a blender; blend until smooth. Pour into a freezer-safe dish; cover and freeze several hours. Heat apple cider thoroughly in a large saucepan; pour into serving mugs. Add one tablespoon frozen mixture to each mug; stir until melted. Makes 24 servings.

Lollipop Cookies

Jessica Parker
Mulvane, KS

Great party treats or a just-for-fun snack!

18-1/2 oz. pkg. vanilla
   cake mix
1/3 c. oil

2 eggs
20 to 24 wooden popsicle sticks
16-oz. tub favorite frosting

Combine cake mix, oil and eggs together; drop by rounded
tablespoonfuls 3 inches apart on ungreased baking sheets. Insert
top inch of a wooden stick into each mound of dough; bake for 8 to
11 minutes in a 375-degree oven. Cool completely; frost. Makes about
2 dozen.

Cathedral Cookies

Ann Bonito
Lima, OH

A special Christmas treat for the chocolate-lovers in our family.

12-oz. pkg. chocolate chips
4 T. margarine
6 T. egg substitute
2 T. oil
2 c. powdered sugar

1 t. vanilla extract
10-1/2 oz. pkg. colored mini
   marshmallows
1-1/2 c. chopped nuts
24 graham crackers, crushed

Melt chocolate chips and margarine in a double boiler; set aside. Mix
egg substitute and oil in a large mixing bowl; blend in sugar and
vanilla. Stir in chocolate mixture; fold in marshmallows and nuts.
Shape dough into six, 2" diameter logs; roll in graham crackers. Wrap
in wax paper; chill overnight. Slice into 1/4-inch slices to serve. Makes
2 to 3 dozen.

Vintage glass prisms (from chandeliers) make sparkly Christmas
tree ornaments...pick up a few at the flea market.

Sweets for Santa

Candy Cane Puffs

Kristine Marumoto
Sandy, UT

Just right for giving, these look so pretty in a Christmas tin.

2-1/2 c. all-purpose flour
1/4 t. salt
1/2 c. butter, softened
1 c. powdered sugar
1 egg

1/2 t. peppermint extract
1 t. vanilla extract
8-oz. pkg. white chocolate chips
1/2 c. peppermint candies, finely
  crushed

Combine flour and salt; set aside. Cream butter and sugar; beat in egg and extracts. Mix into flour mixture using low speed. Wrap dough in plastic wrap; refrigerate for one hour. Shape dough into walnut-size balls; place on lightly greased baking sheets. Bake at 375 degrees for 10 to 12 minutes; cool. Melt white chocolate chips in a double boiler; dip cooled cookies into melted chocolate. Roll in crushed peppermint candy; set on wax paper until hardened. Makes about 4 dozen.

Have a Christmas Eve buffet without the fuss. Split the meal into courses and let guests choose a course to bring...spend less time in the kitchen and more with family & friends!

Double Chocolate Chip Cookies

Ann Fehr
Trappe, PA

*Use 2 cups chocolate chips and 2 cups peanut butter chips
for a tasty variety.*

4 c. chocolate chips, divided   2 eggs
3/4 c. butter   2 c. all-purpose flour
3/4 c. sugar   1 t. baking soda

Melt 2 cups chocolate chips in a double boiler; set aside to cool. Cream butter, sugar and eggs together; blend in dry ingredients and melted chocolate. Fold in remaining chocolate chips. Drop by rounded teaspoonfuls onto ungreased baking sheets; bake at 350 degrees for 8 to 9 minutes. Makes 4 dozen.

Keep cookie cutters handy for holiday cookie baking...store them on
the countertop in an old-fashioned pantry jar.

Aunt Rosie's Butter Cookies

Lynn Darda
Winamac, IN

*Top with your favorite frosting and sprinkle with holiday jimmies
or brightly colored sugars.*

1-2/3 c. all-purpose flour
1/4 t. salt

1 c. butter, softened
1/3 c. sugar

Sift flour and salt together; set aside. Cream butter and sugar together
in a large mixing bowl; add flour mixture, mixing well. Cover;
refrigerate dough 2 to 3 hours. Shape dough into a roll; wrap in wax
paper and refrigerate overnight. Slice dough into 1/4-inch slices; place
on ungreased baking sheets. Bake at 325 degrees for 14 minutes; cool
on wire racks completely. Makes about 3 dozen.

Celebrate early with St. Nicholas Day on December 6th!
Each family member sets out their shoes on the night
of the 5th...St. Nick will fill the shoes of those
who've behaved with treats and small presents.

Coffee Hermits

Pamela Raybon
Edna, TX

*A wonderful addition to office parties, cookie trays or
to give to your favorite coffee-lover.*

1/2 c. shortening
1 c. brown sugar, packed
1 egg
2 T. water
1-1/2 c. all-purpose flour
2 t. instant coffee granules
1/2 t. baking soda

1/2 t. cinnamon
1/4 t. salt
1/4 t. nutmeg
1/2 c. raisins
1/2 c. chopped nuts
1/2 c. chocolate chips

Cream shortening and brown sugar together; blend in egg. Add water;
set aside. Sift next 6 ingredients together; mix into sugar mixture. Fold
in remaining ingredients; drop by rounded teaspoonfuls onto lightly
greased baking sheets about 2 inches apart. Bake at 350 degrees for
10 minutes. Makes about 5 dozen.

Rocking Around the Christmas Tree

Traveling for the holidays? Have little ones leave Santa a note
with instructions telling him where you'll be visiting
the night before Christmas!

We Wish You a Merry Christmas

Family, friends and presents galore,
a Christmas feast is what's in store!

Early Morning Breakfast

Kringle

Linda Blackburn
Miller, SD

*Grandma made these Norwegian treats for us often...now my mom
makes them for the grandkids at Christmas and birthdays!
They're so yummy served warm with butter.*

1-1/2 c. sugar
1 c. shortening
2 eggs
1/8 t. salt
1-1/2 c. buttermilk

1 t. vanilla extract
1 t. baking powder
5 c. all-purpose flour
1/2 t. nutmeg

Mix ingredients together in order given; wrap dough in plastic wrap
and chill. Roll tablespoonfuls of dough out on a lightly floured surface
into 8-inch ropes. Shape ropes into figure eights; place on ungreased
baking sheets. Bake at 400 degrees for 8 to 10 minutes or until
golden. Makes 6 to 8 dozen.

Yes, Virginia,
there is a Santa Claus.
- Francis P. Church

Early Morning Breakfast

Cappuccino Sticky Buns

Delinda Blakney
Bridgeview, IL

*These sweet, nutty buns are perfect for breakfast
or as a late-night snack!*

1/2 c. maple syrup
1/4 c. butter
1 envelope instant
   cappuccino mix

1/2 c. chopped pecans
7-1/2 oz. tube refrigerated
   biscuits

Combine syrup and butter in a small saucepan; bring to a boil over
medium heat. Stir in cappuccino mix; reduce heat to low. Continue
to stir and cook for one minute; pour into an 8" round baking pan.
Sprinkle with pecans; arrange biscuits over the top. Bake at
400 degrees for 12 to 15 minutes, or until golden. Invert onto
a rimmed serving platter; serve immediately. Makes 8 servings.

Remember the magic of each
year with a Christmas memory
album. Fill it to the brim
with plenty of photos,
letters to Santa, best-kept
secrets and the
biggest surprises!

American Breakfast Skillet

Denise Pawlak
Grinnell, IA

My husband created this hearty recipe...we have it on
Sunday mornings at least once a month.

12-oz. pkg. maple-flavored
   sausage
2 c. sliced mushrooms
28-oz. pkg. frozen, diced
   potatoes with green pepper
   and onion

6 to 8 eggs, beaten
Garnish: shredded Cheddar
   cheese

Brown sausage with mushrooms in a 10" skillet; drain and set aside.
Cook potatoes until golden; add in eggs. Stir and heat until eggs are
scrambled; add sausage and mushroom mixture. Spoon onto plates;
garnish with cheese. Makes 4 servings.

Christmas Eggs

Wendy Smithee Windal
Burkburnett, TX

My mom always served these eggs with cinnamon rolls
and mini sausages.

1 T. butter
1 doz. eggs
10-3/4 oz. can cream of chicken
   soup

salt and pepper to taste

Melt butter in a 10" skillet. Meanwhile, whisk eggs and soup together
in a mixing bowl; salt and pepper to taste. Pour egg mixture into
skillet; scramble eggs until done. Makes 6 to 8 servings.

Ham & Eggs Casserole

Diana Chaney
Olathe, KS

*Serve with a pitcher of fresh-squeezed orange juice
for a delicious breakfast.*

1 round loaf sourdough bread
4 to 5 eggs, beaten
1/4 c. evaporated milk
1/4 t. garlic salt
1/4 t. pepper

1/3 c. cooked, smoked ham, diced
1/2 c. shredded mild Cheddar cheese

Slice bread horizontally into one-inch thick slices; set aside. Coat a 1-1/2 quart casserole dish with non-stick vegetable spray; cover the bottom with one slice of bread, reserving remaining bread for use in another recipe. Mix eggs, evaporated milk, garlic salt and pepper together; pour over bread slice. Sprinkle ham over the top; cover and refrigerate overnight. Uncover and layer cheese over mixture; bake at 375 degrees for 20 to 22 minutes. Serves 6.

One doesn't forget the rounded wonder in the eyes of a boy
as he comes bursting upstairs on Christmas morning and finds the
fire truck of which, for weeks, he has scarcely dared to dream.
- Max Lerner

Blueberry-Croissant French Toast

Jo Ann

A simple twist on a favorite breakfast classic.

1 c. half-and-half
2 eggs
1/3 c. sugar
1/4 c. milk
1 t. cinnamon
1/4 t. salt

8 T. blueberry preserves, divided
4 croissants, sliced horizontally
1/2 c. butter
1 pt. blueberries
Garnish: maple syrup

Mix the first 6 ingredients together in a 13"x9" glass baking dish; whisk well and set aside. Spread 2 tablespoons preserves each on 4 croissant halves; top with remaining halves. Arrange croissants on top of cream and egg mixture; turn to coat. Set aside until liquid is absorbed, about 45 minutes; turn often. Melt butter in a 10" skillet over medium-high heat; add croissants. Heat until golden on both sides; transfer to serving plates. Add blueberries to same skillet; heat thoroughly, about 3-1/2 minutes. Spoon berries over croissants; garnish with maple syrup. Makes 4 servings.

When visiting friends during the holidays, slip an ornament
onto their tree with a small gift tag...when they take down
the tree, it'll be a thoughtful after-Christmas surprise.

Amazing French Toast

Amy Blanchard
Holly, MI

This delicious breakfast is perfect for busy weekday mornings...you prepare it the night before!

1 c. corn syrup
1 c. brown sugar, packed
1 c. butter
12 slices raisin bread

6 eggs
2 c. milk
1 t. vanilla extract

Bring corn syrup, brown sugar and butter to a boil in a saucepan over medium heat; boil for 5 minutes. Pour into a buttered 13"x9" baking pan. Layer half the bread slices on the mixture; top with remaining bread slices and set aside. Beat eggs, milk and vanilla together; pour over bread. Cover with aluminum foil; refrigerate overnight. Uncover; bake at 350 degrees for 45 minutes. Serve with remaining glaze as syrup. Makes 12 servings.

Christmas is here, merry old Christmas, gift-bearing, heart-touching, joy-bringing Christmas, Day of grand memories, King of the year!
-Washington Irving

Bran & Raisin Muffins

Jody Pressley
Charlotte, NC

*Filled with plump raisins, these sweet muffins are perfect
for breakfast or tucked into a lunch box.*

2 c. whole-grain wheat flake
   cereal with raisins
1-1/2 c. milk
1-1/2 c. all-purpose flour
1 t. baking soda

1/4 t. salt
1 egg
1/2 c. brown sugar, packed
2 T. butter, melted

Mix cereal with milk; set aside. In a large mixing bowl, combine
remaining ingredients; stir in cereal mixture. Fill lightly greased or
paper-lined muffin tins about 2/3 full with batter; bake at 350 degrees
for 20 to 25 minutes. Makes 12.

A "coupon" for a home-cooked meal or free babysitting will be a
welcome gift for far-away college students or busy parents!

Christmas Morning Muffins

Mary Jones
North Lawrence, OH

To save time, pour batter into muffin tins the night before, cover with a damp towel and refrigerate until ready to bake.

2 eggs, beaten
3/4 c. milk
1/2 c. oil
2 c. all-purpose flour

1/3 c. sugar
3 t. baking powder
1 t. salt

Blend eggs, milk and oil together; add remaining ingredients, stirring until just moistened. Fill paper-lined or lightly greased muffin tins 2/3 full; bake at 400 degrees for 20 minutes or until golden. Remove from pan; spread topping on while warm. Serve at once. Makes 12.

Topping:

1/2 c. butter, melted
1 c. sugar

2 t. cinnamon

Combine ingredients; whisk until creamy.

For a personal gift tag, string fresh cranberries on wire and shape into the recipient's initial...so sweet!

Baked Oatmeal

Laura Strausberger
Roswell, GA

Need a quick breakfast? Make this hearty treat ahead of time,
slice and freeze until needed.

2 c. long-cooking oats,
   uncooked
1-1/2 t. baking powder
1/2 t. cinnamon
1/2 t. salt

2 c. milk
2 eggs, beaten
1/2 c. applesauce
1/2 c. brown sugar, packed
Garnish: vanilla yogurt

Combine oats, baking powder, cinnamon and salt; stir in milk, eggs,
applesauce and brown sugar. Pour into a greased 2-quart casserole
dish; bake at 325 degrees for 45 minutes. Serve hot, topped with a
spoonful of yogurt. Serves 6.

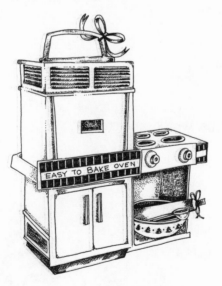

Send snowflake shadows dancing around the room by gently taping
dark paper snowflakes to the inside of a lamp shade. So pretty!

Sausage & Blueberries

Jessica Smith
Ventura, CA

You may want to double the blueberry
sauce...it's always a hit!

2 c. all-purpose flour
1 t. baking powder
1/2 t. baking soda
1/2 c. margarine
3/4 c. sugar

1/4 c. brown sugar, packed
2 eggs
1 c. sour cream
1 lb. ground sausage, browned
1 c. blueberries

Sift flour, baking powder and baking soda together in a medium mixing bowl; set aside. Cream margarine in a large mixing bowl; add sugars, mixing well. Add eggs, one at a time, beating well after each addition; mix flour mixture and sour cream alternately into sugar mixture. Fold in sausage and blueberries; pour into an ungreased 13"x9" baking pan. Cover; refrigerate overnight. Bake at 350 degrees for 35 to 40 minutes or until golden on top; serve warm with blueberry sauce. Makes 10 servings.

Blueberry Sauce:

1/2 c. sugar
2 T. cornstarch
1/2 c. water

2 c. blueberries
1/2 t. lemon juice

Combine sugar and cornstarch in a medium saucepan; add water and blueberries. Heat and stir over medium heat until thickened and bubbly; continue heating for 2 minutes. Remove from heat; stir in lemon juice. Cool slightly before serving. Makes 2 cups.

Quick & easy candlelight! Fill simple goblets with water, top with a floating candle and line up along the mantel.

Grandma's Waffles

Dean Avery
Dexter, MI

Sprinkle with fresh berries and powdered sugar
for an extra touch of sweetness.

1/4 c. sugar
2 eggs
1/8 t. salt
1 t. baking soda

1/2 t. nutmeg
1 qt. buttermilk
3 c. all-purpose flour
2 T. shortening, melted

Blend first 5 ingredients together; mix in buttermilk. Add flour; blend well. Stir in shortening; heat on an ungreased waffle iron following the manufacturer's instructions. Makes 12 to 15.

Maple-Blueberry Sauce

Janet Lumbert
Cumberland Center, ME

Make 2 batches...one to pour over breakfast waffles
and one to pour over ice cream.

1/4 c. brown sugar, packed
1 T. cornstarch
1/2 c. maple syrup
1/2 c. water

2 c. blueberries
1 T. lemon juice
1/8 t. nutmeg

Combine brown sugar and cornstarch in a saucepan; gradually whisk in maple syrup and water. Heat over medium heat until thick and bubbly; stir in blueberries, lemon juice and nutmeg. Heat until berries are warmed through; cool slightly before serving. Makes 3 cups.

Banana-Berry Muffins

Gianni Bertolone
Cleveland Heights, OH

Try substituting one cup chocolate chips for blueberries...yum!

2 c. all-purpose flour
1 T. baking powder
1 t. salt
1/3 c. brown sugar, packed
1 c. frozen blueberries,
    partially thawed

1/2 c. oil
1/3 c. milk
1 egg
2 bananas, mashed
3 t. sugar
1 t. cinnamon

Combine first 4 ingredients together; gently stir in blueberries until coated. In another mixing bowl, mix oil, milk and egg; set aside. Fold bananas into flour mixture; add liquid mixture. Stir until just moistened; fill greased muffin tins 2/3 full. Sprinkle with sugar and cinnamon; bake at 400 degrees for 20 minutes. Makes 12.

Surprise your four-legged friends this year...hang stockings for them and fill with home-baked treats, new squeaky toys and personalized dishes!

Sour Cream Twists

Emily Flake
Colorado Springs, CO

My mom used to greet me at the door with these when I came home from school, but they're perfect anytime!

1 pkg. active dry yeast
1/4 c. warm water
1 c. shortening, melted
1 c. sour cream
1 t. salt

1 t. vanilla extract
2 eggs
3-1/2 c. all-purpose flour
1 c. sugar
1 t. cinnamon

Sprinkle yeast over warm water; set aside. Combine shortening, sour cream, salt and vanilla; blend in yeast mixture and eggs. Add flour; mix well. Cover and refrigerate at least 2 hours; roll out dough into a 15"x10" rectangle. In a separate mixing bowl, combine sugar and cinnamon; sprinkle dough generously. Fold rectangle in thirds, like a letter; roll dough out again into another rectangle, without unfolding dough. Sprinkle again; repeat folding, rolling and sprinkling until sugar mixture is gone. Cut final rectangle into 4"x1" strips; twist 2 times. Bake on greased baking sheets at 375 degrees for 10 to 12 minutes; spread on glaze while warm. Serves 6.

Glaze:

1 c. powdered sugar
1 t. vanilla extract

1/4 c. margarine, melted

Blend ingredients together until smooth and creamy.

Spend some time finding ornaments that reflect
special friends' personalities or interests.
Date and sign them for heartfelt gifts.

Early Morning Breakfast

Overnight Coffee Cake

Linda Zell
Delavan, WI

*This moist coffee cake needs to be refrigerated overnight
before baking, but it's well worth the wait!*

2 c. all-purpose flour
1 t. baking powder
1 t. baking soda
1 t. cinnamon
1/2 t. salt

2/3 c. butter, softened
1 c. sugar
1/2 c. brown sugar, packed
2 eggs
1 c. buttermilk

Sift first 5 ingredients together; set aside. Cream butter and sugars
in a large mixing bowl; add eggs. Mix in dry ingredients alternately
with buttermilk; spread evenly in a greased and floured 13"x9" baking
pan. Sprinkle with topping; cover with aluminum foil and refrigerate
overnight. Uncover and bake at 350 degrees for 45 minutes or until a
toothpick inserted in the center removes clean; cool. Makes about
16 servings.

Topping:

1/2 c. brown sugar, packed
1/2 c. chopped walnuts

1 t. cinnamon
1/4 t. nutmeg

Toss ingredients together until walnuts are well coated.

Spiced Sweet Potato Pancakes

Delinda Blakney
Bridgeview, IL

*A tasty way to enjoy wholesome sweet
potatoes...my three boys love 'em!*

1-1/4 c. all-purpose flour	1 egg
3 T. brown sugar, packed	1 t. vanilla extract
1-1/2 t. baking powder	1 t. lemon zest
1/3 t. cinnamon	2 T. butter, divided
3/4 c. milk	Garnish: warm maple syrup
1/2 c. sweet potatoes, cooked	
and mashed	

Mix first 4 ingredients together; add milk, sweet potatoes, egg, vanilla
and zest. Stir until just moistened; set aside. Melt one tablespoon
butter on a hot griddle; pour batter by 1/4 cupfuls onto hot griddle.
Heat until tops are bubbly; turn and cook until golden. Keep warm
until serving; serve with warm syrup. Makes 10 to 12.

For the coziest holiday
fires, stack wood in a
criss-cross pattern to
allow plenty of room
for air circulation.
Toss in a few scented
pine cones when
starting...smells
like home.

Early Morning Breakfast

Oatmeal Pancakes

Tammy Harri
Eaton Rapids, MI

*Try serving with thick-sliced bacon
and fresh fruit salad...so hearty!*

2 eggs
2 T. oil
1 c. whole-grain bread flour
1 c. long-cooking oats,
   uncooked
1-1/2 t. baking powder

1/2 t. salt
3/4 c. orange juice
1/2 c. chopped nuts
2 T. butter

Blend eggs and oil together; set aside. In a medium-size bowl, combine dry ingredients. Stir in egg mixture; add enough orange juice to create a thick batter. Fold in chopped nuts; mix well. Melt butter on a griddle; pour batter by 1/4 cupfuls onto griddle. Heat until bubbles form around edges; turn and heat until golden. Makes 8 to 10.

German Pancakes

Heather Berry
Roseburg, OR

Delicious topped with your favorite jam or preserves.

1/2 c. all-purpose flour
1/2 c. milk
1/8 t. salt
2 eggs

2 T. butter
Garnish: butter and powdered
   sugar

Mix first 4 ingredients together; set aside. Heat an 8" cast iron skillet in a 350-degree oven until warmed, about 3 to 5 minutes; coat with butter. Pour batter into skillet; return to oven and bake 10 minutes or until golden. Remove from oven; slice and place on serving plates. Garnish with butter and powdered sugar. Serves 2.

Cranberry-Orange Scones

Dayna Hansen
Junction City, OR

During the busy holiday season, my sisters and I always pick one morning to hold our annual "sisters' brunch." We each share special moments, gifts and yummy dishes. This is a favorite!

2 c. all-purpose flour
10 t. sugar, divided
1 T. orange zest
2 t. baking powder
1/2 t. salt
1/4 t. baking soda
1/3 c. chilled butter

1 c. dried cranberries
1/4 c. plus 1 T. orange juice, divided
1/4 c. half-and-half
1 egg
1 T. milk
1/2 c. powdered sugar

Combine flour, 7 teaspoons sugar, orange zest, baking powder, salt and baking soda; cut in butter with a pastry cutter until coarse crumbs form. In a small bowl, stir cranberries, 1/4 cup orange juice, half-and-half and egg together; add to flour mixture until a soft dough forms. Knead 6 to 8 times on a lightly floured surface; pat into an 8-inch circle. Cut into 8 wedges; separate wedges and place on an ungreased baking sheet. Brush with milk; sprinkle with remaining sugar. Bake at 400 degrees for 12 to 15 minutes; cool slightly. Combine powdered sugar and remaining orange juice; drizzle over warm scones. Makes 8.

I will honor Christmas
in my heart, and try to
keep it all the year.
- Charles Dickens

Maple-Pecan Brunch Ring

Leslie Williams
Americus, GA

A sweet & simple way to make a tasty treat for guests.

3/4 c. chopped pecans
1/2 c. brown sugar, packed
2 t. cinnamon
2 17.3-oz. tubes refrigerated
    extra-large flaky biscuits

2 T. butter, melted
1/2 c. maple syrup

Combine pecans, brown sugar and cinnamon; set aside. Split each biscuit in half horizontally; brush half of the biscuit halves with butter and sprinkle with half the sugar and cinnamon mixture. Arrange this half of the biscuits in a circle on an ungreased baking sheet; overlap each biscuit slightly and keep within 2 inches from the edge of the baking sheet. Brush remaining biscuit halves with butter; sprinkle with remaining sugar and cinnamon mixture. Arrange a second ring just inside the first ring, overlapping edges a bit; bake at 350 degrees for 30 to 35 minutes or until deep golden. Remove to wire cooling rack; cool 10 minutes. Brush with maple syrup; slice and serve. Makes about 12 servings.

Host a themed gift exchange this holiday...give winter warm-ups
like hats & gloves or spread cheer with holiday CD's
and shiny, new ornaments.

Fireside Soups & Breads

Wild Rice Bread

Jenny Baker
Waynesburg, PA

*This bread is perfect to snack on while stringing cranberries
and popcorn for the Christmas tree.*

2-1/2 c. all-purpose flour,
   divided
1 pkg. active dry yeast
1/2 t. salt
1 c. water

2 T. butter
2 T. maple syrup
1 egg
1 c. prepared wild rice
1/2 c. chopped pecans

Combine 1-1/2 cups flour, yeast and salt in a large mixing bowl; mix
well and set aside. Heat water, butter and syrup in a one-quart
saucepan over medium heat until mixture reaches 120 to 130 degrees
on a candy thermometer; add to flour mixture. Blend in egg; beat at
medium speed until smooth, about 2 to 3 minutes. Stir in remaining
flour, rice and pecans by hand; mix well. Spread batter in a greased
2-quart casserole dish; cover and let rise until double in bulk, about
30 minutes. Bake at 375 degrees for 30 to 35 minutes; remove from
casserole dish immediately. Cool. Makes 8 servings.

Christmas isn't a season. It's a feeling.
- Edna Ferber

Chili Chicken Stew

Nancy Hauer
Rifle, CO

This stew is a fall tradition in our family...we love it so much, we usually make two pots.

1 onion, chopped
1 T. oil
3 to 4 boneless, skinless chicken
    breasts, cooked and chopped
1 green pepper, seeded
    and sliced
1/2 t. garlic, minced
28-oz. can stewed tomatoes,
    undrained

2 15-oz. cans pinto beans,
    undrained
3/4 c. picante sauce
1 t. cumin
1 t. chili powder
Garnishes: sour cream, grated
    Cheddar cheese, sliced
    black olives

Sauté onion in oil until soft; add chicken, green pepper and garlic. Heat thoroughly. Pour tomatoes into a slow cooker; mash into large pieces. Add chicken mixture; mix in remaining ingredients. Stir to combine; heat on low setting for 4 to 6 hours. Serve garnished with sour cream, grated Cheddar cheese and sliced black olives. Makes 6 servings.

Save those wish lists from little ones each year...a special gift for when they're all grown up.

Williamsburg Cornbread

Carol Hickman
Kingsport, TN

Try this cornbread with chili or a favorite bean soup.

1 c. self-rising cornmeal
2 eggs, beaten
1 c. sour cream

8-oz. can creamed corn
1/2 c. shortening

Blend first 4 ingredients together; set aside. Melt shortening in a 10" skillet; pour into cornmeal mixture, stirring well. Spread cornmeal batter back into same skillet; bake at 400 degrees for 30 minutes. Makes 8 to 10 servings.

5-Hour Beef Stew

Peggy Earley
Midlothian, VA

Serve with a loaf of crusty bread for a hearty meal that makes the house smell oh-so good!

1-1/2 lbs. stew beef, cubed
3 stalks celery, chopped
3 carrots, chopped
1 onion, chopped

8-oz. can tomato sauce
salt and pepper to taste
1 T. quick-cooking tapioca,
   uncooked

Place ingredients in a 1-1/2 quart casserole dish in the order listed; bake at 250 degrees for 5 hours. Makes 6 servings.

Fireside Soups & Breads

Stay-at-Home Stew

Lisa Ashton
Aston, PA

Send the little ones off to school, toss these ingredients together on the stove and then settle in for an undisturbed day of gift wrapping knowing dinner has been taken care of already.

1 lb. stew beef, cubed
1 onion, chopped
1 c. carrots, chopped
2 stalks celery, chopped
1 c. peas
3 potatoes, peeled and cubed

1 t. salt
1/4 t. pepper
1 bay leaf
10-3/4 oz. can tomato soup
3/4 c. water

Combine all the ingredients together in a 2-quart casserole dish; cover and bake at 275 degrees for 5 hours. Remove bay leaf before serving. Serves 5 to 6.

Kids will enjoy decorating the table at holiday dinners. Just cover their table with a tablecloth of plain paper and add a jar of crayons as the centerpiece...memories in the making!

Spud-tacular Soup

Rhonda Douthit
Horse Shoe, NC

So warm & cozy on a winter's day...try topping it
with diced onion and crumbled bacon.

2 stalks celery, sliced	3/4 t. seasoned salt
1 onion, chopped	1/2 t. dried thyme
2 T. margarine, melted	1/2 t. dried rosemary
6 potatoes, peeled and cubed	1/8 t. garlic powder
2 carrots, sliced	1/8 t. pepper
3 c. water	2 c. milk
5 chicken bouillon cubes	1 c. Cheddar cheese, grated

Sauté celery and onion in margarine in a large stockpot until tender;
add next 9 ingredients. Cover and simmer until vegetables are tender,
about 30 minutes; remove from heat. Coarsely mash vegetables; add
milk and cheese. Return to heat, stirring until cheese melts. Makes
10 servings.

The most splendid gift, the most marveled and magic, is the gift
that has not yet been opened. Opaque behind wrapping or
winking foil, it is a box full of possibilities.
- George Easterbrook

Fireside Soups & Breads

Crab Bisque

Brad Sprague
Powell, OH

*This warm and creamy soup is perfect when company's
coming...serve extra cayenne at the table
for guests who like it spicy!*

1 onion, chopped
1 stalk celery, chopped
1 carrot, chopped
1 tomato, chopped
1 head garlic, cloves peeled
   and halved
2 T. olive oil
2 T. fresh tarragon, chopped
2 T. fresh thyme, chopped
1 bay leaf

8 peppercorns
cayenne pepper to taste
1 c. dry Sherry
4 c. chicken broth
1/4 c. tomato paste
1/2 c. whipping cream
1-1/2 T. cornstarch
2 T. water
3 6-oz. cans crabmeat,
   undrained

Sauté first 6 ingredients together until onion is soft; drain and add to a
6-quart stockpot. Add next 6 ingredients; simmer, stirring occasionally,
until most of the liquid is evaporated, about 5 minutes. Pour in broth;
simmer, uncovered, for one hour, stirring occasionally. Pour mixture
through a fine sieve into a large saucepan; discard solids. Whisk in
tomato paste; simmer until reduced to 3 cups, about 10 minutes. Add
cream; simmer 5 minutes. Stir cornstarch and water together in a
small bowl; stir into bisque until thickened, about 2 minutes. Add
crabmeat with juices; simmer 2 to 3 minutes or until meat is warmed
through. Makes 4 to 6 servings.

Recycle those old Christmas
cards...try making bookmarks
and postcards or have the
kids cut and paste for
easy ornaments!

Cranberry Soda Bread

Marci Meyer
Whitewright, TX

*Try raisins or dried, diced apples in place of
the cranberries for variety.*

1/2 c. long-cooking oats,
  uncooked
1-3/4 c. buttermilk
1/3 c. honey
2 T. oil

3 c. all-purpose flour
1/2 c. whole-wheat flour
1-1/2 t. salt
1 t. baking soda
1 c. dried cranberries

Combine oats, buttermilk, honey and oil; set aside. Mix remaining
ingredients together in a large mixing bowl; make a well in the center.
Add buttermilk mixture; stir until just moistened. Let dough rest for
5 minutes; turn onto a lightly floured surface. Knead for 30 to
45 seconds; divide dough in half. Shape each half into a round loaf;
cut a shallow slit down the center of each loaf. Bake on a greased and
lightly cornmeal-dusted baking sheet at 400 degrees for 20 minutes;
reduce oven temperature to 375 degrees and continue baking for
25 more minutes. Makes 2 loaves.

When vacationing throughout the year, look for
Christmas ornaments for the tree. Come December, they're
sure to bring great memories of family travels and fun!

Smoky Pumpkin Soup

Catherine White
Sacramento, CA

You've never had pumpkin like this before!

6 slices bacon, crisply cooked
   and crumbled, drippings
   reserved
6 c. pumpkin, peeled and
   chopped
4 T. butter

6 c. beef broth
1/2 c. Marsala wine or beef
   broth
1 t. dried thyme
salt and pepper to taste
Garnish: roasted pumpkin seeds

Sauté pumpkin in reserved bacon drippings and butter for 15 minutes,
stirring occasionally; add broth. Reduce heat and simmer, covered,
until pumpkin is tender, about 30 minutes; remove from heat. Add
wine or broth, thyme, salt and pepper; purée in batches until smooth.
Return to stockpot; add bacon. Simmer for about 10 minutes; serve
immediately sprinkled with pumpkin seeds. Makes 6 servings.

At Christmas, play and make good cheer,
for Christmas comes but once a year.
- Thomas Tusser

Golden Butter Rolls

Norma Maiwald
Lohrville, IA

*Butter is better in this recipe...it's not only easy to make
but also freezes very well.*

1-1/2 to 2 c. all-purpose flour,
    divided
1 pkg. plus 2 t. instant dry yeast
1/2 c. sugar
1 t. salt
1-1/2 c. milk
1 c. butter
3 eggs, beaten and divided

Combine 1-1/2 cups flour, yeast, sugar and salt together; set aside.
Heat milk and butter in a small saucepan to 120 to 125 degrees on a
candy thermometer; remove from heat. Mix into flour mixture; add
2 eggs, mixing well. Add enough remaining flour to make a light
dough; knead 4 to 6 minutes. Place dough in a lightly greased bowl;
turning once to coat both sides. Cover and let double in bulk. Divide
into 4 equal parts; roll each into a 13-inch circle. Cut into 8 wedges;
roll each up crescent roll-style. Place on a lightly greased baking sheet;
set aside to double in bulk. Brush tops lightly with remaining egg;
bake at 375 degrees for 15 to 17 minutes. Makes 16 servings.

A holiday gift just in time...give a New Year's basket
filled with party hats, festive noisemakers, glittery confetti
and plenty of treats too!

Fireside Soups & Breads

Minnesota Wild Rice Soup

Elaine Wilcox
Austin, MN

This recipe will feed a crowd...perfect for holiday gatherings!

1 onion, diced
4 stalks celery, diced
1-1/2 c. carrots, shredded
1/3 c. butter
3 49-1/2 oz. cans chicken broth
3 c. cooked chicken, cubed
1/4 t. pepper

1-1/8 t. poultry seasoning
50-oz. can cream of mushroom
   soup
50-oz. can cream of chicken
   soup
4 c. prepared wild rice
1 c. whipping cream

Sauté onion, celery and carrots in butter in a large stockpot for 5 to 7 minutes; add broth, simmering until tender. Add remaining ingredients; heat thoroughly without boiling. Makes about 35 servings.

For whimsical holiday napkin rings, twist a length of foil star garland around each napkin...so easy!

Gruyére Potato Gratin

Kathy Unruh
Fresno, CA

*Serve this cheesy, creamy side dish with roasted chicken or turkey
and everyone will be asking for seconds!*

2 lbs. Yukon Gold potatoes,
   peeled and sliced
6-oz. pkg. Gruyére cheese,
   coarsely grated

salt and pepper to taste
1 c. milk
1 c. whipping cream
nutmeg to taste

Heat potatoes in salted boiling water in a 5-quart saucepan for
4 minutes; drain. Layer 1/3 of the potatoes in a buttered 3-quart
casserole dish; sprinkle with 1/2 cup cheese. Repeat layers one time;
top with remaining potatoes. Salt and pepper to taste; set aside. Pour
milk and cream into a heavy saucepan; heat to just boiling. Whisk in
nutmeg; pour over potatoes. Sprinkle with remaining cheese; bake at
400 degrees for 30 minutes or until top is golden and potatoes are
tender. Makes 4 servings.

A vintage muffin tray makes a delightful holiday candleholder. Place
a scented votive candle in each cup and surround them with
cranberries or rosehips.

Holiday Soufflé

Melissa McCune
Joshua, TX

Sprinkle with buttered bread crumbs for a crunchy topping.

3 T. all-purpose flour
3 T. butter, melted
1/2 t. salt
2 c. cottage cheese
3 eggs, beaten

6-oz. pkg. shredded Cheddar
 cheese
10-oz. pkg. frozen spinach,
 thawed

Combine all the ingredients in the order listed; pour into a 1-1/2 quart casserole dish. Bake at 350 degrees for one hour. Serves 6.

Add a little color to this year's snowman...fill spray bottles
with colored water and spritz for rosy cheeks
and brightly colored clothing!

Crispy Veggie Salad

Stacie Allison
Fredericksburg, VA

This recipe is guaranteed to tickle your taste buds!

2 lbs. carrots, peeled and
    thinly sliced
1 c. green pepper, chopped
2 c. celery, finely chopped
1 bunch scallions, chopped

1-1/2 t. celery seed
1 c. cider vinegar
1 c. sugar
1/4 c. oil

Add carrots to boiling water; heat until crisp-tender and drain.
Combine carrots, green pepper, celery, scallions and celery seed in a
shallow dish; set aside. Heat remaining ingredients in a small
saucepan until sugar is dissolved; pour over vegetables. Cover
and refrigerate overnight. Makes 12 servings.

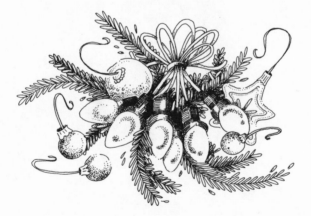

Give friends a memory-making basket complete with everything
needed to record special moments...a blank scrapbook,
decorative-edged scissors, photo corners along with
metallic and colored pens.

Delicious Cheesy Cornbread

Barbara Robertson
Chuckey, TN

*This seems like a lot of ingredients, but it's easy
to prepare and so-o-o good.*

7-oz. pkg. cornbread mix
1 onion, chopped
1/2 c. margarine, melted
1 c. cottage cheese
3 eggs, beaten

10-oz. pkg. frozen broccoli,
    thawed
1 c. shredded Cheddar cheese
1 c. shredded mozzarella cheese

Mix all the ingredients together; spread in a 13"x9" greased baking pan. Bake at 400 degrees for 30 to 35 minutes or until golden on top; set aside for 5 minutes before serving. Makes 18 servings.

Christmas waves a
magic wand over
this world, and behold,
everything is softer
and more beautiful.
- Norman Vincent Peale

Gingered Fruit Salad

Judy Wolf
Corning, IA

*Fruit salad is oh-so versatile...serve this delicious dish
as a side, dessert or snack!*

2 oranges, peeled and sectioned
2 apples, cored, peeled
   and chopped
2 peaches, pitted, peeled
   and sliced

1 c. strawberries, hulled
   and halved
1 c. peach or vanilla yogurt
2 T. brown sugar, packed
1/2 t. ground ginger

Toss fruit together in a large serving dish; set aside. Combine
remaining ingredients; whisk until creamy. Pour over fruit; stir until
coated. Serves 8.

Running to the window, he opened it, and put out his head.
Golden sunlight; Heavenly sky; sweet fresh air;
merry bells...oh glorious! Glorious!...Christmas Day!
- Charles Dickens

Mandarin Orange & Almond Salad *Marilyn Golema*
Wyandotte, MI

I like to double this recipe for potlucks and guests still ask for more!

2 bunches Romaine lettuce
1 sweet onion, sliced

2 15-oz. cans mandarin
   oranges, drained

Tear lettuce into bite-size pieces; mix gently with onion and oranges in a large serving bowl. Fold in sugared almonds; pour dressing on top. Makes 8 servings.

Sugared Almonds:

4-1/2 to 5-oz. pkg. sliced
   almonds

4 T. sugar

Add almonds and sugar to a non-stick skillet; stir constantly over medium heat until sugar is dissolved and almonds are well coated. Remove from heat; cool in a glass or ceramic bowl.

Dressing:

1/2 c. oil
4 T. vinegar
4 T. sugar

2 T. dried parsley
1 t. salt

Shake ingredients together until well blended.

Add whimsy to windows this season...tie a pine cone onto each end of a ribbon for festive curtain tie-backs.

Stuffed Acorn Squash

Jill Turney
Des Plaines, IL

Try it with chopped walnuts too!

1 acorn squash, halved and
    seeded
1/3 c. bread crumbs
1/4 c. brown sugar, packed
3 T. chopped pecans

2 T. butter, softened
1/2 apple, cored, peeled
    and diced
3 T. sweetened, dried cranberries

Place both halves of squash cut-side down in a baking dish filled with
1/4 to 1/2 inch of water; bake at 325 degrees for 30 to 45 minutes, or
until tender. Combine remaining ingredients together in a small bowl;
set aside. Remove squash halves from oven; turn cut-side up. Spoon
filling into centers; bake for an additional 15 to 20 minutes. Serves 2.

Dress up the mantel with chunky scented candles tied with
homespun or sheer ribbon...arrange with fruit and holiday greenery.

Sweet Potato Casserole

Demetria Stevenson
Port Orange, FL

*The sweet, crunchy topping on this casserole makes it a hit
at the holiday dinner table!*

40-oz. can yams
1/2 c. sugar
1/2 c. milk
2 eggs
1 t. cinnamon
1 t. nutmeg

1 t. vanilla extract
1 c. brown sugar, packed
1/2 c. all-purpose flour
1/3 c. pecan pieces
1/4 c. butter, melted

Mix first 7 ingredients together; spread in a greased 2-quart casserole
dish. In another mixing bowl, combine remaining ingredients until
crumbly. Spread evenly over yam mixture; bake, uncovered, at
350 degrees for 45 minutes. Makes 6 servings.

Let this Christmas be one of happiness, and the New Year
be radiant with hope and filled with the impulse
of doing something for somebody every day.
- Joe Mitchell Chapple

Baked Potato Salad

Sara Ferko
Washington, PA

*Serve this cheesy salad with pork chops and steamed
broccoli for a hearty meal.*

8 to 10 potatoes, baked
   and cubed
1/2 c. mayonnaise
1/2 c. onion, chopped

1 lb. American cheese, grated
1/2 c. bacon bits
salt and pepper to taste

Arrange potatoes in a 13"x9" baking dish; set aside. Combine
mayonnaise and onion together; spread over potatoes. Sprinkle with
cheese and bacon bits; salt and pepper to taste. Bake at 325 degrees
for 30 minutes. Makes 8 to 10 servings.

Greet guests with Christmas memories! Pull out childhood holiday
photos and enlarge them on a color photocopier...decoupage onto
an old wooden sled. Seal with polyurethane and
tie on a shimmering bow.

Corn Casserole

Pat Davis
Yorkville, IL

*An easy-to-prepare potluck dish...it's best after it's
set aside for an hour or so.*

16-oz. can corn, undrained
16-oz. can creamed corn
1 c. elbow macaroni, uncooked
1/2 c. butter, melted

salt and pepper to taste
3/4 c. pasteurized process
   cheese spread, cubed

Combine ingredients in a 2-quart casserole dish; cover and bake, at
425 degrees for 15 minutes. Uncover, lower temperature to
350 degrees and bake another 45 minutes. Stir and serve. Makes
8 servings.

A Christmas family-party!
We know nothing in nature more delightful!
- Charles Dickens

Sweet Pineapple Slaw

Cathy Clemons
Narrows, VA

This unusual mixture is truly delicious and a family favorite.

1 head cabbage, shredded
2 carrots, peeled and shredded
20-oz. can pineapple tidbits,
 drained
1/4 c. sweet onion, chopped
1/2 c. mayonnaise

1/3 c. frozen whipped topping,
 thawed
2 T. sugar
2 T. fresh parsley, chopped
1/2 t. hot pepper sauce
1/2 c. chopped pecans, toasted

Combine first 4 ingredients in a large serving bowl; set aside. Mix remaining ingredients except for the pecans in another bowl; gently toss with cabbage mixture. Cover and chill for one hour; sprinkle with pecans before serving. Serves 6.

Experience the magic of the first snowfall of the season...gather
little ones and snuggle up under a cozy blanket to watch.

Mushrooms & Asparagus Sauté

Gail Prather
Bethel, MN

Brings back fond memories of my Spring garden and reminds me to start checking my mailbox for next year's garden catalogs.

1 lb. asparagus spears, trimmed	2 T. Dijon mustard
water	1/4 t. pepper
1/4 c. butter	1/8 t. salt
2 c. sliced mushrooms	1/2 t. garlic, minced

Place asparagus spears in a 10" skillet; add enough water to cover. Bring to a boil over medium heat until crisp-tender; drain and return asparagus to skillet. Add remaining ingredients; stir well. Heat over medium heat until heated through. Serves 6.

Tasty Poppy Seed Dressing

Sandy Bernards
Valencia, CA

A favorite when poured on a salad of Romaine lettuce, strawberries, raspberries and kiwi.

1 banana, mashed	1 T. lemon juice
1/2 c. sour cream	1 t. dry mustard
1/2 c. mayonnaise	1/2 t. salt
1/2 c. sugar	2 t. poppy seed

Purée all ingredients except poppy seed in a blender until smooth; stir in poppy seed. Store in refrigerator. Makes about 1-3/4 cups.

Make a festive drum...just wrap an empty coffee can or oatmeal container with bright paper and attach gold cord. So fun for a gift package!

Bowtie Pasta Salad

Angie Daniel
Ponca City, OK

*This salad may be made a day or two ahead, covered
and stored in the refrigerator.*

16-oz. pkg. bowtie pasta, cooked
2 cucumbers, chopped
4 roma tomatoes, chopped
1 onion, chopped
1 green pepper, seeded and
   chopped
3/4 c. oil
1-1/2 c. sugar

1-1/2 c. vinegar
2 t. mustard
1 t. salt
1 t. pepper
1 t. dried parsley
1 t. garlic, minced
1 t. seasoned salt

Rinse pasta in cold water; drain. Pour into a large serving bowl; set
aside. Gently mix vegetables together; fold into pasta. Whisk all
remaining ingredients together; pour over pasta mixture. Toss lightly;
cover and refrigerate overnight. Makes 12 servings.

Enjoy the great outdoors while gathering holiday decorations...take a
nature hike to collect greenery, holly berries and pine cones.

Party Cucumbers

LaVerne Fang
Joliet, IL

These are great as a snack or as a side dish!

1 c. sour cream
2 T. cider vinegar
1 T. sugar
1/4 c. fresh dill, chopped
1/2 t. salt
1/4 t. white pepper

1 t. celery seed
2 cucumbers, peeled and
   thinly sliced
1 sweet onion, thinly sliced
Garnish: fresh dill, chopped

Blend first 7 ingredients together; gently stir in cucumbers and onion. Cover and refrigerate at least 2 hours; sprinkle with dill before serving. Serves 4.

Spicy Mushrooms

Mary Gildenpfennig
Harsens Island, MI

A side dish that complements steak and pork very well.

2 T. olive oil
1 to 1-1/2 t. crushed red pepper
   flakes
1/4 t. teriyaki sauce

1-1/2 T. sugar
1 T. red wine vinegar
1/2 t. ground ginger
1-lb. pkg. sliced mushrooms

Combine all ingredients except sliced mushrooms in a saucepan: bring to a boil. Reduce heat; add mushrooms. Simmer for 20 minutes; serve warm. Makes 6 to 8 servings.

Kids can help make personalized giftwrap! Help them cut pictures
of flowers, animals and holiday images from magazines,
then glue onto packages wrapped in solid-color paper.

Christmas Dinner

Ham Steak with Cider Glaze

Gail Prather
Bethel, MN

This is one of those easy, serve-on-an-extra-busy-day kind of suppers. Great with a salad and baked potato!

1 to 2-lb. ham steak, thickly
   sliced
1 c. apple cider
1/4 c. brown sugar, packed

1/4 c. Dijon mustard
1/4 c. honey
1/2 t. liquid smoke

Place ham steak in an ungreased 13"x9" baking pan; set aside. Mix remaining ingredients together; pour over ham steak. Bake at 350 degrees for 30 minutes, basting often. Serves 6.

Jo Ann,
Happy Holidays!
Vickie

How clever! When making homemade bread for Christmas dinner, use a warm bowl to help speed the rising process...simply fill a bowl with hot water, let rest one minute, then empty and dry the bowl before adding dough.

Dressed-Up Holiday Stuffing

John Boyd Brandon
Jemez Springs, NM

My mother gave me this basic recipe 25 years ago and, over the years, I've added my own touches...either way, it's simply delicious!

2 24-oz. loaves white bread
2 6.2-oz. pkgs. long-grain and
   wild rice, prepared
20 to 25 green onions, chopped
3 to 4 c. celery, chopped
2 c. slivered almonds

3 eggs, beaten
salt and pepper to taste
1 t. minced garlic
dill weed to taste
1-1/2 c. butter, melted

Tear bread into bite-size pieces; place in a very large bowl. Add rice, green onions, celery and almonds; pour eggs over mixture. Mix well with your hands; mix in salt, pepper, garlic and dill weed. Pour butter over dressing; mix again with your hands. Place in a deep 13"x9" glass baking dish; bake uncovered at 350 degrees for one hour. Serves 9 to 12.

What a festive way to show off vintage buttons!
Hot glue them onto a foam ball, then top with a
homespun bow for a whimsical, handmade ornament.

Sour Cream Pot Roast

Anita Manninen
Portsmouth, OH

Our favorite is to serve this roast over a
heaping mound of buttered noodles.

2 to 4-lb. chuck roast
1 onion, sliced
1 t. oil
salt and pepper to taste

1 clove garlic, minced
2 c. sour cream
water
1 to 2 T. cornstarch

Brown chuck roast in a Dutch oven; remove to platter. Sauté onion slices in Dutch oven with oil; remove to bowl. Return roast to Dutch oven; sprinkle with salt, pepper and garlic. Spread sour cream and onion slices on top; pour water around, not on, roast until 3/4 up the sides. Cover and simmer until roast is fork-tender, about 2 hours; remove roast only to serving platter, scraping sour cream and toppings back into Dutch oven. In a small bowl, whisk cornstarch into one cup of water; add to Dutch oven. Heat over low heat until thickened; pour over roast before serving. Makes 8 to 10 servings.

Sugared fruit is a cheerful way to add sparkle to a centerpiece. Just brush apples, pears and plums with a thin mixture of meringue powder and water, roll in coarse sugar and let dry.

Chicken & Dumplings

Elizabeth Andrus
Gooseberry Patch

It was tradition to rise very early Sunday morning and prepare the makings of a meal that could cook slowly while the family attended church. Upon returning home, the air would be filled with the wonderful aromas of the afternoon dinner.

1 c. all-purpose flour	2 14-oz. cans chicken broth
1 t. salt	1 onion, sliced in wedges
2 t. paprika	2 t. dried parsley
4 to 6 boneless, skinless chicken breasts	2 c. biscuit baking mix
1/4 c. oil	2/3 c. milk

Combine flour, salt and paprika; coat chicken. Heat oil in a 10" skillet over medium heat; brown both sides of chicken until golden. Drain; reduce heat. Stir chicken broth, onion and parsley together in a small bowl; pour over chicken. Cover tightly; simmer on low heat for 3 hours. Mix biscuit baking mix and milk in a mixing bowl with a fork until just moistened; drop by heaping tablespoonfuls into skillet. Increase heat to medium; cook, covered, for 10 minutes. Uncover and cook 10 more minutes; remove chicken and dumplings to a serving platter. Serve drippings as gravy. Makes 4 to 6 servings.

Tuck a note and a dollar bill or two into a balloon for young relatives who live far away. Mail it inside a card with instructions to blow it up and pop for a surprise!

Best-Ever Meat Loaf

Amanda Simmons
Butler, PA

*Made with ingredients you already have on hand, this meat loaf
is as easy as it is tasty.*

1-1/2 lbs. ground beef
1/2 c. seasoned bread crumbs
1 onion, finely chopped
1 egg, beaten
1-1/2 t. salt
1/4 t. pepper

16-oz. can tomato sauce, divided
1/2 c. water
3 T. vinegar
3 T. brown sugar, packed
2 T. mustard
2 T. Worcestershire sauce

Mix ground beef, bread crumbs, onion, egg, salt, pepper and 1/2 cup
tomato sauce together; form into a loaf and place in an 8"x8" greased
pan. Combine remaining tomato sauce and all other ingredients; pour
over loaf. Bake at 350 degrees for 1-1/4 hours; baste occasionally.
Makes 8 servings.

For yummy-smelling, spiced pomanders, use a tapestry needle
to pierce a design into oranges, then press cloves into the holes.

Christmas Dinner

Melt-in-your-Mouth Rolls

Jerilyn Anderson
Provo, UT

These rolls are the perfect accompaniment to any meal!

3/4 c. plus 1 t. sugar, divided
1/2 c. warm water
2 T. active dry yeast
1 c. butter-flavored shortening
1 c. boiling water

1 c. cold water
4 eggs, beaten
2 t. salt
8 c. all-purpose flour, divided

Dissolve one teaspoon sugar in water; sprinkle yeast over it and set aside. Cream shortening and remaining sugar; blend in boiling water. Add cold water, yeast mixture, eggs and salt; mix well. Add flour, 4 cups at a time; mix well. Let dough rise for one hour; divide into thirds. Roll each third into a circle; cut into 12 wedges. Roll each wedge up crescent roll-style. Cover with plastic wrap that has been sprayed with non-stick vegetable spray; let rise another hour. Bake on ungreased baking sheets at 365 degrees for 15 to 18 minutes. Makes 3 dozen.

Onion-Pepper Rice

Cheri Maxwell
Gulf Breeze, FL

This recipe uses teriyaki sauce but it's down-home good!

1 lb. bacon, chopped
1 sweet onion, chopped
2 green peppers, seeded
    and chopped

6 c. prepared long-grain rice
3 T. teriyaki sauce
2 T. sugar
salt and pepper to taste

Crisply cook bacon; add onion and peppers. Sauté vegetables until tender, about 6 minutes; do not drain. Stir in rice; add remaining ingredients, heating thoroughly. Makes 8 servings.

Ham for a Houseful

Kathy Grashoff
Fort Wayne, IN

*So juicy and sweet...make hot ham sandwiches
with the leftovers, if there are any!*

2 20-oz. cans crushed
  pineapple, drained
2 c. brown sugar, packed
1/4 c. honey

1 T. dry mustard
1 t. ground cloves
2 4 to 5-lb. fully cooked
  boneless hams

Combine all ingredients except the hams in a large saucepan; heat
over medium heat until sugar dissolves, about 5 minutes. Stirring
constantly, heat until liquid reduces and mixture thickens, about
10 more minutes; remove from heat to cool. Score surface of hams in
a diamond pattern; insert meat thermometer into center of ham. Place
hams in a roasting pan; cover and bake at 325 degrees for one hour.
Uncover; spoon glaze over hams. Bake 45 minutes to one hour longer
or until meat thermometer reads 140 degrees; baste every 15 minutes.
Both hams together make about 32 servings.

For cozy firelight without the mess, fill a vintage serving tray
with pillar candles and colored glass beads.
Set in the hearth for a romantic glow.

Ham Sauce

Caroline Booth
Salt Lake City, UT

Serve over your holiday ham as a special treat.

1-1/2 T. dry mustard
1/2 c. sugar
1/8 t. salt

1/2 c. vinegar
2 eggs, beaten
1 c. whipping cream

Combine mustard, sugar and salt; stir in vinegar. Add eggs; mix well. Pour into a double boiler after water has come to a boil; stir constantly until thickened. Remove and cool. Blend whipping cream until slightly thickened; stir into mustard mixture. Makes 1-1/2 cups.

Kids and parents can share in the spirit of giving year 'round. Have the kids make coupons to weed flower beds or mow the lawn together when the weather turns warm...so thoughtful for an elderly neighbor.

Barbecued Beef

Frances Beavers
Land O' Lakes, FL

Serve this saucy shredded beef on toasted hoagie buns
with a side of fries or onion rings.

4 to 5-lb. pot roast or chuck
    roast
1 onion, chopped
2 T. butter
2 T. cider vinegar
2 T. brown sugar, packed
4 T. lemon juice

1 c. catsup
1/2 c. fresh parsley, chopped
1/2 T. mustard
1/2 c. water
3 T. Worcestershire sauce
salt and pepper to taste
hot pepper sauce to taste

Cook meat in a covered roasting pan at 300 degrees for 4 to 5 hours or until meat is tender and registers 160 degrees on a meat thermometer. Shred with a fork and set aside. Sauté onion in butter until soft; add remaining ingredients. Simmer for 30 minutes; add beef. Heat until warmed through; serve heaped on buns. Makes 12 to 18 servings.

Create a personalized calendar for your family!
Use old and new pictures alike for each month and be
sure to add your own holidays and celebrations.

Christmas Dinner

Pork Goulash

Karen Barineau
Aliso Viejo, CA

Serve with dumplings or boiled potatoes.

4 onions, chopped
1/4 c. oil
1 T. paprika
3-lb. pork roast, cubed
1 T. dried marjoram
1 T. tomato paste

1 clove garlic, pressed
1 t. salt
1 c. beef broth
1 t. lemon juice
1 t. all-purpose flour
1 c. sour cream

Sauté onions in oil; blend in paprika. Add pork, marjoram, tomato paste, garlic, salt and broth; simmer, covered, until meat is tender, about 1-1/2 hours. Remove pork; pour sauce through a sieve discarding solids. Return sauce to saucepan; stir in lemon juice. Mix flour and sour cream together in a small bowl; whisk into sauce. Add pork; warm thoroughly without boiling. Makes 6 servings.

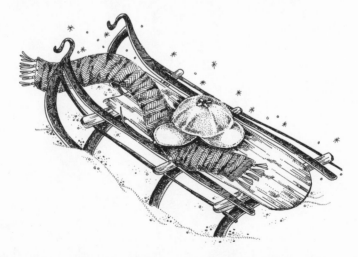

Throw an impromptu sledding party for the first snowfall...gather
with friends & neighbors to enjoy some fun and then
head back home for a cozy fire and hot cocoa.

Creamy Chicken & Noodles

Sherri Hagel
Spokane, WA

*For an unbeatable pair, serve this dish with fresh
buttermilk biscuits...delicious!*

4 boneless, skinless chicken
   breasts, cubed
2 cloves garlic, chopped
2 T. olive oil
10-3/4 oz. can cream of
   chicken soup
1/2 c. mayonnaise
1/4 c. milk

1/4 t. dried rosemary
1 t. poultry seasoning
4-oz. can mushrooms, drained
salt and pepper to taste
1/8 t. dried parsley
2 c. egg noodles, cooked
   and drained

Sauté chicken and garlic in oil until juices of chicken run clear when
pierced with a fork; add remaining ingredients except for noodles. Heat
until hot; add noodles, stirring until warmed. Serves 6.

Welcome guests by hanging a "family wreath" on the door.
Hang a single ornament representing each member of
the family on a simple evergreen wreath, then tie
with a bow...don't forget the family pet!

Christmas Dinner

Chicken with Mushroom Sauce
Noelle McDonald
McKinney, TX

Adjust the amount of hot pepper sauce to your family's taste.

6-oz. pkg. wild rice, prepared
3 whole chicken breasts, split
6 T. butter or margarine, melted
   and divided
1 t. salt
1/4 t. paprika
1/4 t. pepper

1/2 c. onion, chopped
8-oz. pkg. sliced mushrooms
10-3/4 oz. can cream of
   mushroom soup
1/2 t. hot pepper sauce
1/4 c. chicken broth

Spread rice in an ungreased 13"x9" baking dish; arrange chicken on top skin-side up. Combine 4 tablespoons butter, salt, paprika and pepper together; baste over chicken. Bake chicken and rice at 350 degrees for one hour; baste with butter mixture every 15 minutes. In a 10" skillet, combine remaining butter, onion and mushrooms; sauté until onion is soft and mushrooms are golden, about 5 minutes. Add soup, hot sauce and broth; heat thoroughly. Spoon over chicken and rice before serving. Makes 3 servings.

What could be sweeter than a gumdrop tree? Poke tree branches into a sand-filled pail and then press plump gumdrops onto the end of each twig. Tie a gingham bow around the pail and enjoy!

Make-Ahead Mashed Potatoes

Pat Landrum
Highland Heights, KY

An easy way to make mashed potatoes for your holiday dinner!

10 potatoes, peeled and cubed
1 clove garlic
1 c. sour cream
8-oz. pkg. cream cheese,
  softened

1/4 c. onion, chopped
salt and pepper to taste
2 t. butter, melted
Garnish: paprika

Boil potatoes and garlic in a large saucepan until tender; drain and mash. Add sour cream, cream cheese and onion; mix thoroughly. Spread into an ungreased 2-quart casserole dish; cool. Cover and refrigerate for 24 hours; bring to room temperature. Top with melted butter; sprinkle with paprika. Bake at 350 degrees for 30 minutes. Makes 6 to 8 servings.

Spinach Rolls

Janet Pastrick
Gooseberry Patch

*Busy day ahead? Count on this easy, slow-cooker recipe to make
a meal the whole family will love.*

1 lb. ground beef
3 slices bread, toasted
  and crushed
2 onions, chopped
1 egg
1 t. salt

1/4 t. pepper
1/2 t. dried marjoram
1/8 t. nutmeg
16 to 20 spinach leaves
1 c. beef broth
2 T. butter

Combine beef, bread crumbs, onions, egg and seasonings; set aside. Boil spinach leaves for 2 to 3 minutes; drain. Place one heaping tablespoon meat mixture on each spinach leaf. Fold ends together toward center; roll tightly. Place in a slow cooker; add broth. Dot with butter; cover and cook on low for 6 to 8 hours, adding additional broth if necessary. Serves 4 to 6.

Beef Stroganoff

Jennifer Scott
Bear, DE

Serve over your favorite noodles.

1 c. onion, thinly sliced
3 T. oil, divided
3 c. sliced mushrooms
1-1/2 lb. beef flank steak, thinly
    sliced across grain

3/4 c. steak sauce
1/2 c. sour cream
Garnish: fresh parsley, chopped

Sauté onion slices in one tablespoon oil for 3 minutes in a 12" skillet; add mushrooms. Heat until tender; drain and remove to platter. Brown beef in remaining oil in skillet; add onions and mushrooms. Mix in steak sauce; bring to a boil. Reduce heat to low; simmer for 15 minutes. Remove from heat; stir in sour cream. Serve immediately. Garnish with parsley. Makes 4 servings.

Puzzle cookies make sweet treats! Cut a 4"x4" square of cookie dough, then cut into irregular shapes. Separate pieces and bake, frost and reassemble in a gift box or on a serving plate...guests will have fun putting this treat back together.

Linzer Tarts

Vickie

*Delicious with other jam flavors too...try blackberry,
strawberry or even gooseberry!*

1-1/4 c. butter, softened
2/3 c. sugar
1-1/2 c. almonds, ground
1/4 t. cinnamon

2 c. all-purpose flour
1/4 c. plus 1 T. raspberry jam
Garnish: powdered sugar

Cream butter and sugar together until light and fluffy; blend in
almonds, cinnamon and flour, 1/2 cup at a time. Shape dough into a
ball; wrap in wax paper and chill for one hour. Roll out half the dough
on a lightly floured surface to 1/8-inch thickness; cut into 2-1/2 inch
circles. Continue with remaining dough; cut out a small heart or other
shape from the center of half of the circles. Place on ungreased baking
sheets; bake at 325 degrees for 10 to 15 minutes or until lightly
golden. Cool on wire rack about 20 minutes; spread tops of solid
cookies with jam; place a cut-out cookie on top, pressing lightly to
form a sandwich. Sprinkle with powdered sugar. Makes one dozen.

Hosting a dinner party
for family & friends?
Hang a homespun stocking
filled with goodies
on the back of each chair
for instant country charm!

Santa's Whiskers Cookies

Meghan Chryst
Powell, OH

Cookies sprinkled with different colored sugars look so yummy arranged on a festive cookie plate!

1/2 c. shortening
1/2 c. butter, softened
1 c. sugar
1/4 c. sour cream
2 c. all-purpose flour
1/4 t. baking soda

2 t. cinnamon
1/4 t. nutmeg
1/4 t. ground cloves
Garnish: assortment of colored sugars

Cream shortening, butter and sugar together; add sour cream and set aside. Mix remaining dry ingredients together; blend into sugar mixture. Pat into a 1/4-inch thick rectangle on wax paper; freeze. When solid, slice thinly into desired lengths; place on ungreased baking sheets. Sprinkle with colored sugars; bake at 350 degrees until golden, about 6 to 8 minutes. Makes 4 to 6 dozen.

Fill a vase with peppermint candies to anchor a
white pillar candle...a pretty (and easy!) holiday centerpiece.

Fudgies

Rita Nickerson
Mocksville, NC

*Makes a stiff dough, but it's quick & easy
to mix in a food processor.*

1/2 c. shortening	1/3 c. baking cocoa
1 t. vanilla extract	1/8 t. salt
1 c. powdered sugar	2 T. milk
1 c. all-purpose flour	1/2 c. chopped nuts

Cream shortening until fluffy; blend in vanilla and powdered sugar.
Combine flour, cocoa and salt in another mixing bowl; blend into sugar
mixture. Add milk; fold in nuts. Drop by teaspoonfuls about 2 inches
apart onto ungreased baking sheets; bake at 325 degrees for about
18 minutes. Cool on a wire rack. Makes about 2 dozen.

Pass on holiday spirit with a good winter deed!
Shovel the driveway and sidewalk for a neighbor.

Butterscotch-Nut Bars

*Julie Carlson
Mount Vernon, OH*

*These gooey bars are so irresistible, you won't be able
to eat just one!*

2 c. all-purpose flour
1 c. brown sugar, packed
1 c. butter, melted
1 T. vanilla extract
1/4 T. salt
1 egg yolk

12-oz. pkg. butterscotch chips
1/3 c. corn syrup
1 c. butter
1/2 c. chopped walnuts
1/2 c. chopped pecans
1/2 c. macadamia nuts

Combine first 6 ingredients together; press into an ungreased
13"x9" baking dish. Bake at 350 degrees for 25 minutes; cool. While
cooling, heat butterscotch chips, corn syrup and butter together in a
double boiler until melted and smooth; pour over crust. Sprinkle nuts
over the top; press gently into melted mixture. Refrigerate at least one
hour before serving. Makes 24 servings.

Holiday placemats are a great gift for grandparents.
Have the kids put together a collage of photos and drawings then
cover with clear contact paper...a gift that always brings smiles!

Christmas Pie

Caroline Wildhaber
Dayton, OR

*If you take this festive pie to a holiday party, be sure to take copies
of the recipe...everyone will want one!*

1/2 c. powdered sugar
8-oz. pkg. cream cheese,
   softened
1-1/2 c. frozen whipped topping,
   thawed

9-inch graham cracker crust
1 c. raspberries
1 c. water, divided
1 c. sugar
3 T. cornstarch

Blend powdered sugar and cream cheese together until smooth; fold in
whipped topping. Spread in pie crust; set aside. Place raspberries and
2/3 cup water in a saucepan; simmer for 3 minutes. Whisk sugar,
cornstarch and remaining water together in a small bowl until smooth;
add to raspberry mixture. Boil for one minute; remove from heat. Cool
for 5 to 7 minutes; pour over cream cheese mixture. Refrigerate until
firm. Serves 8.

Make merry magnets for the fridge! Cut out festive shapes from last
year's Christmas cards, then glue them to mini clothespins and
attach adhesive magnet stripping to the backs.

Happy Holiday Treats

Hugs & Chips Cheesecake

Peggy Pelfrey
AE, APO

Chocolate and cheesecake...so decadent!

2 3-oz. pkgs. cream cheese,
  softened
14-oz. can sweetened condensed
  milk
1 egg

1 t. vanilla extract
1 c. mini chocolate chips
1 t. all-purpose flour
9-inch chocolate cookie pie crust

Blend cream cheese until fluffy; gradually add condensed milk until smooth. Add egg and vanilla; mix well. In a small bowl, toss chocolate chips with flour; stir into cheese mixture. Spread into pie crust; bake at 350 degrees for 35 minutes or until center springs back when lightly touched. Cool; spread with warm chocolate glaze. Serve chilled. Makes 8 servings.

Chocolate Glaze:

1/2 c. mini chocolate chips

1/4 c. whipping cream

Heat and stir ingredients together in a double boiler until melted and smooth.

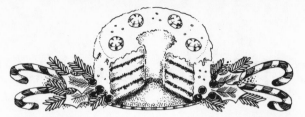

Pumpkin Cookies

Elizabeth VanNatter
Gaston, IN

These moist cookies are perfect for holiday cookie exchanges!

2 c. sugar
2 c. butter
2 eggs
2 t. vanilla extract
15-oz. can pumpkin
4 c. all-purpose flour

2 t. baking powder
2 t. baking soda
1 t. salt
1 t. cinnamon
1 t. nutmeg

Cream first 4 ingredients together; stir in pumpkin. Mix well; set aside.
Sift remaining ingredients together; gradually mix into pumpkin
mixture until well blended. Drop by teaspoonfuls onto ungreased
baking sheets; bake at 350 degrees for 10 to 15 minutes. Cool; frost.
Makes about 8 dozen.

Quick Caramel Frosting:

1/2 c. butter
1/2 c. brown sugar, packed
1/4 c. milk

1 t. vanilla extract
1-3/4 c. powdered sugar

Heat butter and brown sugar until melted and dissolved; remove from
heat. Pour into a mixing bowl; blend in milk and vanilla. Stir in
enough powdered sugar for desired spreading consistency.

Enjoy a new twist on an old favorite! Whip up a quick batch of
no-bake cookies, pour into a wax paper-lined pan and chill.
Cut with cookie cutters to make whimsical,
holiday-shaped cookies.

Happy Holiday Treats

Apple-Cinnamon Bars

Carla Turner
Keizer, OR

*Try topping these with a scoop of vanilla ice cream
and a drizzle of warm caramel sauce.*

1-3/4 c. sugar
2 c. all-purpose flour
3 eggs
1 c. oil
1 t. vanilla extract
1 t. baking powder

1/2 t. salt
1 t. cinnamon
2 c. apples, cored, peeled
  and diced
1 c. chopped nuts
Garnish: powdered sugar

Combine ingredients together in order listed; pour into a greased 13"x9" baking pan. Bake at 350 degrees for 40 to 45 minutes; cool. Sprinkle with powdered sugar; cut into squares. Makes 2 dozen.

Hard-to-buy-for relative?
Make a favorite meal or dessert and surprise them with
a gift to warm their heart and their tummy!

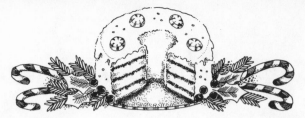

Hot Milk Cake

Beth Montgomery
Knoxville, TN

My Grandmother passed away years ago but one of my favorite memories remains. I loved going to her house and smelling the wonderful aroma of her Hot Milk Cake, made just because she knew I was coming. She handed the recipe down to me and that old, yellow index card is one of my most-cherished and most-requested recipes.

4 eggs, beaten
2 c. sugar
2 c. all-purpose flour
1 c. milk

1/2 c. butter
2 T. baking powder
1 t. vanilla extract
16-oz. tub favorite frosting

Combine eggs and sugar together; add flour, mixing well. In a small saucepan, heat milk and butter together until butter melts; remove from heat and add baking powder and vanilla. Blend into egg mixture. Pour into two, 8" round baking pans; bake at 350 degrees for 30 minutes. Cool and frost. Makes 8 servings.

Make a favorite Christmas recipe booklet! Remove the fronts of old or new Christmas cards and copy family recipes onto them...punch a hole in one corner and tie them together with a sparkly ribbon.

Cherry-Mallow Cake

Terry Cryer
Patterson, CA

Marshmallows rise to the top to become the glaze.

4 c. mini marshmallows
18-1/2 oz. pkg. yellow cake mix

21-oz. can cherry pie filling

Spray the bottom of a 13"x9" baking pan with non-stick vegetable spray; arrange marshmallows evenly in pan. Prepare cake mix according to package directions; pour over marshmallows. Spoon pie filling over the batter; bake at 350 degrees for 45 to 50 minutes. Cool and cut into squares to serve. Makes 15 servings.

For a quick & easy ornament, drizzle glitter glue into the bottom of
a clear ball ornament and twirl to make a swirl design or
fill with winter greenery and confetti "snow."

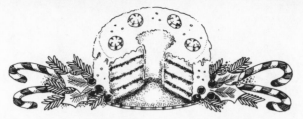

Chocolate-Covered Cherry Cookies
Vicki Wilson
Swansea, IL

*Heat the remaining milk and add in 2 cups chocolate chips and a
little cherry juice, stir until melted and smooth, store in the fridge.
Yummy drizzled over ice cream or pound cake!*

1/2 c. margarine
1 c. sugar
1 egg
1 t. vanilla extract
1-1/2 c. all-purpose flour
1/2 c. baking cocoa
1/4 t. baking powder
1/4 t. baking soda

1/4 t. salt
14-1/2 oz. jar maraschino
   cherries, drained and
   juice reserved
1 c. chocolate chips
1/2 c. sweetened condensed
   milk

Cream margarine and sugar; blend in egg and vanilla. Add dry
ingredients; mix well. Roll into 3/4-inch balls; place on ungreased
baking sheets. Lightly press one cherry in the center of each ball;
set aside. Melt chocolate chips with milk in a double boiler; remove
from heat. Stir in enough cherry juice to make desired spreading
consistency; spread one teaspoonful over each cherry. Bake at
350 degrees for 10 minutes; cool 3 minutes before removing to wire
racks to cool completely. Makes 3 to 4 dozen.

Surprise busy parents by tucking movie tickets into their Christmas
card...the thoughtful "get-away" will be welcome!

Spreading New Year's Cheer

Out with the old and in with the new;
lots of good luck wishes to you!

Cheddar Dip

Pamela Christopher
Pulaski, TN

Enjoy with fresh veggies, buttery crackers and chips.

2 c. sharp Cheddar cheese,
  grated
2 c. sour cream
5 slices bacon, crisply cooked
  and crumbled

3 oz. sun-dried tomatoes,
  chopped
2 T. dried, minced onion
1 T. hot pepper sauce

Mix ingredients together in a serving bowl; cover and refrigerate
8 hours or more. Makes about 4 cups.

Sausage-Cheese Balls

Nita Pilkington
Reeds Spring, MO

Hearty and delicious...serve these on a warming plate.

1-1/2 lbs. ground sausage
10 oz. Colby cheese, grated

2 c. biscuit baking mix

Combine ingredients together; mix well. Shape into walnut-size balls;
bake on ungreased baking sheets at 350 degrees for 20 minutes or
until browned. Serves 4 to 6.

Fare for the Festivities

Pinwheels

Katie Hoover
Norman, OK

Make these oh-so-handy appetizers and you won't miss out on any of the party fun...you prepare them the night before.

10-oz. pkg. frozen chopped
    spinach, thawed
1 c. sour cream
3/4 c. mayonnaise
3-oz. pkg. cream cheese,
    softened
1.4-oz. pkg. dry vegetable
    soup mix

8-oz. can whole water chestnuts,
    chopped
1 bunch green onions, thinly
    sliced
10-1/2 oz. pkg. flour tortillas

Prepare spinach according to package directions; drain well. Combine with next 6 ingredients; spread over tortillas. Roll up and place seam-side down on a baking sheet; cover and refrigerate overnight. Slice into 1/2-inch thick slices. Serves 10 to 12.

Kid's "Champagne"

Wendy Bowman
Bellevue, WA

Toast in plastic champagne glasses!

1 ltr. white grape juice

2 ltrs. ginger ale

Combine; serve well chilled. Makes 12 servings.

Eggless Nog

Erin Moore
El Cajon, CA

This non-dairy recipe is ideal for holiday guests with special diets...it's so delicious, you may never go back to the old way!

4-oz. pkg. instant vanilla
   pudding mix
8 c. soy milk, divided
1/2 c. sugar

2-1/2 t. vanilla extract
1 t. nutmeg
1 t. cinnamon
1 t. ground ginger

Dissolve pudding mix with one cup soy milk; mix until thickened. Add remaining ingredients; blend well. Chill for at least one hour before serving. Makes 8 servings.

Use a funnel to add confetti to balloons before blowing them up.
Give these to guests to pop at midnight for some extra fun!

Burgundy Meatballs

Suzanne Flinn
Bedford, IN

This recipe has become a New Year's favorite in our house!

1-1/2 lbs. ground beef
1 egg, beaten
1-1/2 t. salt
1/8 t. pepper
1/4 c. bread crumbs
1/3 c. milk
2 T. dried, minced onion, divided

1 T. butter
1-1/2 T. all-purpose flour
1/4 t. garlic powder
1 c. beef broth
2 T. tomato paste
1/2 c. raisins
Optional: 1/4 c. burgundy wine

Mix first 6 ingredients together; add one tablespoon onion. Shape into 18 balls; brown in butter in a skillet over medium heat. Remove meatballs; whisk flour and garlic into drippings in skillet. Add remaining onion, beef bouillon, tomato paste, raisins and meatballs; cover and simmer for 10 minutes. Remove meatballs to a hot serving dish; stir wine into remaining sauce in skillet, if desired. Heat thoroughly; pour sauce over meatballs before serving. Serves 4 to 6.

Celebrate the new year early with little ones who can't make it 'til midnight. Get out those noisemakers and toast with sparkling juice!

Pepperoni Balls

Doris Taylor
New Concord, OH

Have bowls of warm pizza sauce or melted butter
seasoned with garlic ready for dipping.

24-ct. pkg. frozen dinner rolls
8-oz. pkg. mozzarella cheese,
   cubed into 24 pieces

1/4 lb. sliced pepperoni
2 T. margarine, melted
2 T. Parmesan cheese, grated

Place frozen dinner rolls in lightly greased muffin cups; cover with
plastic wrap sprayed with non-stick vegetable spray. Let rise 3 to
4 hours. Remove rolls; gently push one piece of mozzarella cheese and
2 slices pepperoni into each dough center. Pinch closed and place
seam-side down into muffin cups; recover with plastic wrap. Let rise
30 more minutes; bake in a 350-degree oven for 10 to 15 minutes or
until golden. Remove from oven. Brush with melted margarine;
sprinkle with Parmesan cheese. Makes 48.

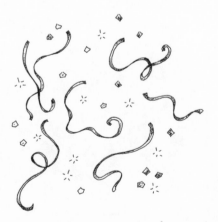

Make homemade confetti using a paper punch and
construction paper. Look for crafty paper
punches in clever shapes too!

Fare for the Festivities

Party Triangles

Phyllis Wittig
Lancaster, CA

These tasty treats never last long!

10-oz. pkg. frozen chopped
   spinach, thawed and drained
2 6-oz. jars marinated artichoke
   hearts, drained and chopped
1 clove garlic, minced

1/2 c. mayonnaise
1/2 c. sour cream
3/4 c. Parmesan cheese, grated
10-oz. pkg. frozen puff pastry,
   thawed

Combine first 6 ingredients together; mix well. Unfold pastry on a
lightly floured surface; roll into a 12-inch square. Cut into sixteen,
3-inch squares. Spoon one teaspoon spinach mixture into the center of
each pastry. Fold pastries over to form triangles; seal with a fork. Place
on an ungreased baking sheet; bake at 350 degrees for 5 to 7 minutes.
Makes 16.

Deviled Eggs

Linda Haiby
Andover, MN

This recipe has a little added zip from the vinegar and
Worcestershire sauce...it's my family's favorite.

12 eggs, hard-boiled and peeled
2 t. Dijon mustard
1/4 t. pepper
1/2 t. salt
1 t. Worcestershire sauce

6 T. mayonnaise-type salad
   dressing
1 T. white vinegar
Garnish: paprika

Slice each egg in half lengthwise; remove yolk to a mixing bowl. Mash
yolks; blend in remaining ingredients except egg whites and paprika
until smooth and fluffy. Spoon mixture into egg white bowls; sprinkle
with paprika. Makes 24.

Hot Cheese Bites

Jan Caudill
Tuscumbia, AL

Double the recipe for a crowd...just bake in a 13"x9" baking dish.

2 eggs, beaten
2 T. all-purpose flour
1 t. salt
1/3 c. milk
4-oz. can green chilies, drained
    and chopped

8-oz. pkg. shredded mozzarella
    cheese
8-oz. pkg. shredded Cheddar
    cheese

Blend eggs, flour, salt and milk together; stir in remaining ingredients.
Spread into a greased 11"x7" baking dish; bake at 350 degrees for
30 minutes. Cool and cut into squares; serve warm. Makes 18.

Cheddar Fondue

Lori Steen
Aloha, OR

Dip bread cubes of all varieties into this dreamy fondue!

1/4 c. butter
1/4 c. all-purpose flour
1/2 t. salt
1/4 t. pepper
1/4 t. mustard

1/4 t. Worcestershire sauce
1-1/2 c. milk
8-oz. pkg. Cheddar cheese,
    grated

Melt butter in a saucepan; whisk in flour, salt, pepper, mustard and
Worcestershire sauce until smooth. Gradually add milk; boil for
2 minutes or until thickened, stirring often. Reduce heat; add cheese,
stirring until melted. Transfer to fondue pot or slow cooker; keep
warm. Makes 2-1/2 cups.

Christmas Brie

Claynette Hemke
Portland, OR

This looks so festive and takes a short time to prepare...serve with lots of crunchy baguette rounds.

8-oz. pkg. Brie cheese
1/2 c. sun-dried tomatoes, minced

1/2 c. fresh parsley, minced
5 cloves garlic, minced
2 T. olive oil

Carefully remove the top crust from the Brie; discard and set cheese aside. Combine remaining ingredients in a microwave-safe bowl; heat until garlic has softened, about 2 to 3 minutes. Spread over top of Brie; heat in the microwave until cheese melts, about 45 seconds to one minute. Makes 8 servings.

Santa Claus is coming to town!

Create a family time capsule! Decorate a coffee can and fill it with some current photos, a newspaper, ticket stubs or childrens' drawings. Seal the capsule and hide it away...a great surprise in years to come!

Grated Onion Tart

Barbara Argotsinger
Storm Lake, IA

*Every year, we make a delightful gourmet dinner with our best friends.
There's plenty of good conversation and fun in the kitchen as we
prepare several courses. This has remained a yearly tradition even
though the main courses have changed.*

1 sheet frozen prepared puff pastry, thawed	1/4 lb. bacon, diced
	3 c. onions, thinly sliced
1/2 c. sour cream	1/4 c. Parmesan cheese, grated

Place pastry on a lightly floured surface; roll out to a 14"x11" rectangle.
Arrange on an ungreased baking sheet; tuck edges under 1/2 inch all
around. Bake at 325 degrees until slightly puffed, about 5 minutes; let
cool. Spread sour cream evenly over the top; set aside. Sauté bacon
and onion until bacon is crisply cooked; drain. Spoon over sour cream
layer; sprinkle with Parmesan cheese. Bake an additional 15 to
20 minutes; cut into squares and serve warm. Makes about 20.

A good beginning makes a good ending.
- English Proverb

Hot Antipasto Squares

Deborah Byrne
Clinton, CT

An easy, no-mess way to enjoy zesty antipasto.

2 8-oz. tubes crescent rolls,
   divided
1/4 lb. cooked ham, thinly sliced
1/4 lb. Swiss cheese, thinly
   sliced
1/4 lb. salami, thinly sliced
1/4 lb. provolone cheese, thinly
   sliced

1/4 lb. pepperoni, thinly sliced
2 eggs, beaten
7-oz. jar roasted red peppers,
   drained and chopped
3 T. grated Parmesan cheese

Unroll one package of crescent rolls; press into an ungreased
13"x9" baking pan, sealing edges. Layer the meats and cheeses in the
order given; lightly press down. Combine eggs, peppers and Parmesan
cheese in a small mixing bowl; pour over pepperoni layer. Unroll
remaining crescent rolls; shape into a 13"x9" rectangle, pressing seams
together gently. Carefully lay it on top of the egg mixture; cover with
aluminum foil. Bake at 350 degrees for 30 minutes; uncover, reduce
heat to 250 degrees and bake an additional 30 minutes. Cool; cut into
squares to serve. Makes 2 dozen.

Punch losing its punch? Keep it from becoming diluted with an
ice ring made of juice! Just freeze cranberry or pineapple juice
in an angel food cake pan and pop out.

Stuffed Strawberries

Barbara Parham Hyde
Manchester, TN

Try using pecans in place of the walnuts for added variety.

20 large strawberries, hulled
  and divided
3-oz. pkg. cream cheese,
  softened

2 T. walnuts, finely chopped
1-1/2 T. powdered sugar

Dice 2 strawberries; set aside. Cut a thin layer from the stem end of remaining strawberries, forming a base. Starting at opposite end of strawberry, slice into 4 wedges being careful not to slice through the base; set aside. Blend remaining ingredients together until fluffy; fold in diced strawberries. Spoon one teaspoonful into the center of each strawberry. Refrigerate until serving. Makes 18.

Invite friends & family to make fun predictions for the upcoming year. Write them down in a scrapbook along with photos from the New Year's celebration. How fun to look back on them next year!

Festive Fruit Tart

Patricia Smith
Douglasville, GA

Top with kiwi, bananas and any other family-favorite fruits.

1/2 c. margarine, melted
1/4 c. powdered sugar
1 c. all-purpose flour
14-oz. can sweetened condensed
   milk
8-oz. pkg. cream cheese,
   softened

1/4 c. lemon juice
1 t. vanilla extract
4 T. cornstarch
2 10-oz. pkgs. frozen
   strawberries, partially
   thawed

Blend margarine with powdered sugar; add flour, mixing well. Press mixture onto a pizza pan. Bake at 350 degrees for 10 minutes; set aside to cool. Mix condensed milk with cream cheese until smooth; blend in lemon juice and vanilla. Spread over cooled crust. In a one-quart saucepan, bring cornstarch and strawberries to a boil; stir constantly until thickened. Spread over cream cheese mixture; refrigerate until firm. Makes 8 to 10 servings.

Light up the dinner table with an individual votive candle and holder at each place setting. Write each guest's name on the holder with acrylic paint and they can take them home as party favors!

Happy New Year Crackers

Leslie Stimel
Gooseberry Patch

Tug heartily on ends to pop in the New Year
with treats and surprises.

scissors
paper towel tube
ruler
wrapping paper

tape
curling ribbon
small candies & toys

Cut tube into four, 3-inch lengths; center 2 lengths next to each other on an 11"x6" piece of wrapping paper, leaving a one-inch space between the lengths. Wrap paper around tubes; secure with tape. Tie one end closed using several strands curling ribbon. Fill tube with candy and toys; tie closed with several strands curling ribbon, using scissors to curl the ribbons on both ends. Repeat with remaining lengths of tube. Makes 2 crackers.

Crafts to Ring in the New Year

Glittery Tea Lights

Mary Murray
Gooseberry Patch

Line up a sparkly row right down your black-tie table.

assorted tea lights
seed beads
mini sequins

paint brush
craft glue
glitter

Remove tea light from metal holder; set candle aside. Spread beads and sequins in a single layer on a flat plate or baking sheet. Paint sides of metal holder with a thin coating of glue; roll in beads or sequins. Sprinkle with glitter, filling in all space between sequins or beads with glitter and shaking lightly to remove excess. Set aside to dry thoroughly. Replace candle once holder is dry.

Beaded Beverage Markers

T.R. Ralston
Gooseberry Patch

*Guests will never lose their glass again with these
beverage markers...they're "charm"ing!*

6-inch lengths 20-gauge multi-
  colored craft wire
needle-nose pliers

wire cutters
assorted beads, charms or
  buttons

Carefully shape a length of wire into a circle; string on desired beads,
buttons and/or charms. Using needle-nose pliers, bend a small hook
on one end of the wire and a loop on the other end. Place around the
stem of a glass; gently hook ends together. Repeat for remaining
glasses, stringing a different bead color or charm on each.

Personalize purchased
stemware with
bead-spangled
beverage markers. At
the end of the evening
guests can take them
home...New Year's Cheer
from you!

Crafts to Ring in the New Year

Good Fortune Favors

Sarah Oravecz
Gooseberry Patch

Good fortune for the new year will smile on everyone at your party with these fun, be-ribboned favors.

scissors
8-1/2"x11" sheets colored paper
calligraphy pen

fortunes or fun quotes
curling ribbon
clear plastic ornaments

Cut strips of paper one to 2" wide, as needed to fit in ornaments, and 8-1/2" long. Using a calligraphy pen, write a fortune or quote on each strip of paper. Roll each fortune into a tight, small scroll and tie with curling ribbon, leaving ends of ribbon long. Place one fortune into each ornament; allow excess curling ribbon to trail out of ornament. Stack the favors in a small tub or glass bowl. Let each guest choose one and read their fortune aloud.

More fun with fortunes!
Write them on slips of paper
for each guest. Place each in a
balloon and give to guests
to pop when the clock
strikes midnight!

Baked Potato Skins

Gloria Kaufmann
Orrville, OH

These are as good as any you can buy...I make a large batch and freeze them and then add the toppings just before serving.

4 potatoes, baked
3 T. oil
2 T. grated Parmesan cheese
1/4 t. salt
1/4 t. garlic powder
1/4 t. paprika
1/8 t. pepper

8 bacon slices, crisply cooked
   and crumbled
1-1/2 c. shredded Cheddar
   cheese
Garnish: 1/2 c. sour cream,
   4 green onions, chopped

Slice potatoes in half lengthwise; remove potato leaving a 1/4-inch shell. Brush skins and shell with oil; sprinkle with Parmesan cheese, salt, garlic powder, paprika and pepper. Arrange shells skin-side up on a greased baking sheet; bake at 475 degrees for 7 minutes. Turn skins over; bake an additional 7 minutes. Sprinkle bacon and Cheddar cheese inside shells; bake 2 minutes longer or until cheese is melted. Garnish with sour cream and onions; serve immediately. Makes about 8 servings.

Remember making paper snowflakes? Revive the
tradition...fold white felt squares into fourths
and cut into snowflake shapes. Use a paper punch
to cut out shapes and stitch onto a stocking.

Hearty Hospitality

Touchdown Taco Dip

Tammy Farmer
Tallassee, TN

Double or even triple for a whole day of New Year's football games!
Serve with bowls of tortilla chips and toasted pita wedges.

16-oz. can refried beans
8-oz. pkg. cream cheese
1-1/4 oz. pkg. taco seasoning
   mix

1 tomato, chopped
1/4 c. onion, chopped
1/2 c. shredded Cheddar cheese
Garnish: sour cream

Spread refried beans over the bottom of a 9" pie pan; set aside. Combine cream cheese and taco seasoning together; spread over beans. Sprinkle with tomato, onion and Cheddar cheese; bake at 375 degrees for 25 to 30 minutes. Dollop with sour cream before serving. Serves 6.

Keep creamy dips and spreads chilled throughout the festivities!
Line a small flowerpot with parchment paper and fill
with dip or spread. Fill a larger flowerpot half-way
with ice and set the smaller pot inside.

Crab Rangoon

Susie Backus
Gooseberry Patch

These are a yummy appetizer for any get-together...also great with your favorite Chinese dish!

8-oz. can imitation crabmeat,
  finely chopped
12 oz. cream cheese, softened
1/4 t. garlic powder

1/4 t. seasoned salt
16-oz. pkg. won ton wrappers
oil for deep-frying

Combine first 4 ingredients in a mixing bowl; mix well. Spoon one teaspoon crab mixture into the center of each won ton; fold corners, completely enclosing filling. Seal final corner of won ton with a touch of water; fry in oil until golden. Makes about 4 dozen.

Oriental Wings

Judy Steinbach
Rancho Cordova, CA

The combination of sweet & spicy makes these wings hard to resist!

10 to 18 chicken wings
1/3 c. soy sauce
2 T. oil
2 T. chili sauce

1/4 c. honey
1/2 t. ground ginger
1/4 t. garlic powder

Place chicken wings in a large bowl; set aside. Combine remaining ingredients; pour over wings. Toss to coat; cover and refrigerate for at least one hour. Pour into an aluminum foil-lined 13"x9" baking pan; bake at 375 degrees for 50 to 60 minutes. Serves 6.

Hearty Hospitality

Sun-Dried Tomato Spread

Peggy VanDomelen
Vancouver, WA

Serve with bread sticks, crackers and tortilla chips.

1/2 c. oil-packed, sun-dried
   tomatoes, drained
14-oz. can artichoke hearts,
   drained and chopped
8-oz. pkg. shredded Swiss
   cheese

1/2 c. sour cream
1/4 c. mayonnaise
1 clove garlic, minced
2 T. grated Parmesan cheese

Combine first 6 ingredients together; mix well. Spread into an ungreased 8"x8" baking dish; sprinkle with Parmesan cheese. Bake at 350 degrees for 20 to 25 minutes. Makes 2-1/4 cups.

For party invites, unroll a party hat, write the details
on the inside and send. Don't forget to sprinkle
some confetti in the envelope!

Onion Pretzels

Shelly Strunk
Clark, NJ

Make several batches to last all day long.

1 c. margarine, melted
1 T. Worcestershire sauce
2 1-1/2 oz. pkgs. dry onion
   soup mix

16-oz. pkg. extra-large pretzels,
broken

Combine margarine, Worcestershire sauce and onion soup mix
together; toss with pretzel pieces until well coated. Spread on a baking
sheet; bake at 325 degrees for 15 minutes. Turn oven off; stir pretzels
again and leave in oven until cool. Serves 6.

Savory Crackers

Lisa Smith
Richmond, IN

Perfect as a snack or sprinkled on top of your favorite soup!

1-oz. pkg. dry ranch dressing
   mix
1/4 c. oil

1/2 t. dill weed
1/4 t. garlic powder
12-oz. pkg. oyster crackers

Combine ranch dressing mix, oil, dill weed and garlic powder; pour
over crackers. Spread on an ungreased baking sheet; bake
at 375 degrees until golden and crispy, about 15 minutes. Place warm
crackers on paper towels to absorb excess oil. Makes 24 servings.

Hearty Hospitality

Dill Dip

Sylvia Schutt
Burkeville, VA

Just right served in a pumpernickel bread bowl!

8-oz. pkg. cream cheese,
    softened
1/2 c. mayonnaise
1/2 c. sour cream
1/4 c. onion, finely chopped

1/4 c. green olives, chopped
2 T. dill weed
1 T. Worcestershire sauce
1 t. hot pepper sauce

Combine all ingredients together well; cover and chill for several hours before serving. Makes 2-1/2 cups.

A hollowed-out squash is a fun way to serve favorite dips...place it on a cut-glass tray and surround with a variety of crackers.

Pineapple Ball

Janice Patterson
Black Forest, CO

*Serve with an assortment of crackers and bread sticks
and watch it disappear!*

2 8-oz. pkgs. cream cheese,
   softened
2 T. green pepper, chopped
2 T. onion, finely chopped
2 t. seasoned salt

1/4 c. crushed pineapple,
   drained
2 T. sugar
2 c. chopped pecans, divided

Mix first 6 ingredients with one cup pecans; shape into a ball. Roll in
remaining pecans; cover with plastic wrap and refrigerate until firm.
Makes about 2-1/2 cups.

For a touch of old-fashioned cheer, use
vintage alphabet blocks to spell out
New Year's greetings on a mantel or buffet.

Hearty Hospitality

Yummy Cider Mix

Anita Wallace
Placerville, CA

A quick mix to have on hand when guests drop by.

1/4 c. butter, softened
1/2 t. cinnamon
1/8 t. nutmeg

4 T. red cinnamon candies
1-1/4 c. brown sugar, packed
1/4 t. ground cloves

Combine ingredients together; store in an airtight container in the refrigerator. To serve, stir one heaping tablespoon mix into one cup of hot apple juice or cider. Makes 24 servings.

A white cotton tablecloth can become a family memento!
Using a paint pen, ask each family member to write a
holiday message, draw a picture and sign
their names with the year.

Cheese Logs

Sally Anderson
Springfield, MN

Make these appetizers ahead of time and freeze until ready to use.

8-oz. pkg. cream cheese,
   softened
2 c. shredded Cheddar cheese
2 c. shredded Swiss cheese
1 t. mustard

1 t. Worcestershire sauce
1 t. paprika
1 t. lemon juice
2 c. chopped nuts

Combine all ingredients together except the nuts; mix well. Divide in half; shape each half into a log. Roll logs in chopped nuts; wrap in plastic wrap and chill until serving. Makes 20 servings.

Have fun with party invitations...hand deliver the details rolled up in a small glass bottle or write them on the "tail" of a party blower.

Hearty Hospitality

Creamy Onion Triangles

Barbara Mitchell
Vacaville, CA

*Cut bread into holiday shapes using mini cookie cutters
for a festive addition to your holiday spread.*

4 green onions, chopped
1/2 c. Parmesan cheese, grated
6 T. mayonnaise

8 slices white bread, crusts
  trimmed

Combine onions, cheese and mayonnaise; set aside. Cut each bread slice into quarters; place on an ungreased baking sheet. Toast one side under the broiler; turn and spread cheese mixture on untoasted side. Return under broiler and broil until bubbly. Makes 32.

Welcome the new year with whimsy...give guests
bubbles to blow when the new year arrives!

Homemade Bread

Donna Turgeon
Nichols, NY

Smells so good while baking that everyone will be gathered in the kitchen to get the first slice!

2 pkgs. instant yeast
5 to 5-1/2 c. all-purpose flour,
   divided
3/4 c. sugar

2 t. salt
3/4 c. oil
2 c. hot water

Combine yeast, 2 cups flour, sugar and salt together in a large mixing bowl; blend in oil. Mix in water with a spoon until dough appears smooth and satiny; gradually add remaining flour until dough pulls away from sides of the bowl. Cover; let stand 10 minutes then knead. Place dough in a greased bowl; let rise 1-1/2 hours. Punch dough down; divide into 2 loaves. Place each loaf in a greased 9"x5" loaf pan; let rise another 1-1/2 hours. Bake at 350 degrees until golden. Makes 16 servings.

Serving homemade herb butter? Roll it into a log, wrap in plastic wrap and place in the fridge to chill. When dinner's ready, simply unroll the plastic and slice into 1/4-inch pieces and place a few slices at each place setting.

Cheeseburger Soup

Lynne Herzberg
Stanley, KS

Try serving in a sourdough bread bowl...less dishes to wash!

3/4 c. onion, chopped
3/4 c. carrots, shredded
3/4 c. celery, diced
1 t. dried basil
1 t. dried parsley
4 T. butter, divided
3 c. chicken broth
4 c. potatoes, peeled and diced

1/2 lb. ground beef, browned
1/4 c. all-purpose flour
2 c. pasteurized process cheese
    spread, cubed
1-1/2 c. milk
3/4 t. salt
1/4 t. pepper
1/4 c. sour cream

Sauté onion, carrots, celery, basil and parsley in one tablespoon butter until vegetables are tender, about 10 minutes; add broth, potatoes and beef. Bring soup to a boil; reduce heat, cover and simmer for 10 to 12 minutes or until potatoes are tender. Melt remaining butter in a small skillet; whisk in flour until bubbly, about 3 to 5 minutes. Add flour mixture to soup; bring to a boil. Heat and stir for 2 minutes; reduce heat to low. Add cheese, milk, salt and pepper; stir until cheese melts. Remove from heat and blend in sour cream; serve warm. Serves 4.

Fill an empty ice bucket with a charming floral arrangement...a clever centerpiece for New Year's Day.

Meatless Minestrone

Anne Messier
Sacramento, CA

Serve sprinkled with freshly grated Parmesan cheese.

1 onion, chopped
2 cloves garlic, chopped
2 carrots, sliced
2 stalks celery, chopped
1/4 c. olive oil
28-oz. can Italian plum
   tomatoes, undrained and
   chopped
2 14-oz. cans chicken broth
1 potato, peeled and thickly
   sliced

1 T. fresh parsley, chopped
2 t. dried basil
1 t. dried oregano
1 t. salt
1/4 t. pepper
15-oz. can kidney beans,
   drained
2 c. cabbage, shredded
1 zucchini, sliced
1/2 c. small shell pasta

Sauté onion, garlic, carrots, and celery in oil in a 4-quart stockpot until tender; add tomatoes, broth, potato, parsley, basil, oregano, salt and pepper. Bring mixture to a boil; reduce heat. Cover and simmer 20 minutes; stir in beans and cabbage. Continue to simmer another 10 minutes; stir in zucchini and pasta. Simmer uncovered 10 minutes or until pasta is done. Serves 4 to 6.

Dress up a holiday dessert table. Fold a large, white sheet of tissue paper several times and cut out a snowflake pattern. Unfold and place over a blue paper tablecloth for a fun, wintry design!

Herb Rolls

Kathryn Harris
Lufkin, TX

*These may be prepared several hours ahead and
refrigerated until ready to bake.*

1/2 c. butter
1-1/2 t. dried parsley
1/2 t. dill weed
1 T. dried, minced onion

2 T. grated Parmesan cheese
10-oz. tube refrigerated
   buttermilk biscuits

Melt butter in a 9" skillet; set aside. Combine herbs and cheese
together; mix into butter. Let stand 15 to 30 minutes. Quarter each
biscuit; coat with herb-butter mixture. Arrange on an ungreased
baking sheet; bake at 425 degrees for 12 to 15 minutes. Serves 4.

To send a message of peace and hope for the new year, set glowing
white tapers in a sand-filled bucket on the front porch.

Fresh Cream of Tomato Soup

Deborah Ludke
Glenville, NY

Snuggle up with this soup on a cold, blustery day.

6 tomatoes, peeled, seeded
   and chopped
1 onion, chopped
1/2 c. butter

1/2 c. all-purpose flour
1 c. half-and-half
salt and pepper to taste
Garnish: oyster crackers

Bring tomatoes and onion to a boil in a stockpot; reduce heat and simmer for 20 minutes. In a small skillet, melt butter; whisk in flour until smooth and bubbly, about 4 minutes. Slowly add half-and-half; whisk until smooth. Add salt and pepper to taste; set aside. Purée half the tomato mixture; pour back into stockpot with remaining half. Stir in the cream mixture; simmer until thoroughly heated but do not boil. Serve in bowls with oyster crackers sprinkled on top. Makes 4 servings.

Carry on a Scandinavian tradition...save the trunk
of the Christmas tree for next year's Yule log!

Sweet Potato & Carrot Soup

*Sandie Hart
Eugene, OR*

If you prefer a thinner soup, add up to 3/4 cup of extra broth.

2 T. butter
2 onions, chopped
2 lbs. sweet potatoes, peeled
　　and cubed
1 lb. carrots, peeled and sliced
5 c. chicken broth

1 t. salt
1-1/4 t. ground ginger
1/4 t. pepper
1 T. lemon juice
Garnish: crystallized ginger,
　　finely chopped

Melt butter over low heat in a large stockpot; add onions. Heat until soft, about 5 minutes; stir occasionally. Add sweet potatoes and carrots; heat, covered, for 5 minutes more. Pour in broth; bring to a boil. Add salt; reduce heat and simmer, partially covered, until vegetables are tender, about 25 minutes. Purée soup in a blender until smooth; return soup to the stockpot. Stir in ground ginger, pepper and lemon juice; reheat until warmed through. Pour into serving bowls; sprinkle with crystallized ginger. Serves 6.

"I love my grandparents because..." Have a little one write down all the reasons they love their grandparents and present the list at the beginning of the new year. Handwritten on special paper and framed, it'll make a truly meaningful gift.

Aunt Ellen's Oatmeal Bread

Wendy Lee Paffenroth
Pine Island, NY

Aunt Ellen is my godmother. Growing up, I always looked forward to her visits during the holidays...and her scrumptious oatmeal bread.

1-1/2 c. boiling water
1 c. quick-cooking oats,
    uncooked
1/4 c. butter
2 pkgs. active dry yeast
1 T. sugar
1/2 c. lukewarm water

1/3 c. molasses
2 t. salt
3-3/4 to 4-1/4 c. bread flour,
    divided
Optional: 1-1/2 c. chopped
    walnuts

Pour boiling water over oats and butter; stir and set aside until lukewarm. In another mixing bowl, dissolve yeast and sugar in lukewarm water; set aside for 10 to 15 minutes. Add molasses to oat mixture; stir in yeast mixture, salt and 1-1/4 cups flour, stirring well. Add walnuts, if desired; stir well. Gradually mix in remaining flour until a stiff dough develops; knead on a lightly floured surface. Place dough in a greased bowl, turning once to lightly coat all sides; cover and let rest until double in bulk. Punch down dough; divide into 2 loaves. Cover and let rest 15 minutes; place in two, greased 9"x5" loaf pans. Let rise again; bake at 400 degrees for 30 to 35 minutes. Makes 16 servings.

Enjoy the serenity of a country setting...ring in the New Year at an old-fashioned bed & breakfast.

Cream of Mushroom Soup

Jennifer Niemi
Kingston, Nova Scotia

Chock-full of mushrooms!

3 T. butter	1/4 t. pepper
2 c. onion, chopped	3 t. dill weed
9 c. sliced mushrooms, divided	4 c. milk
4 c. vegetable broth	1/2 c. whipping cream

Melt butter in a 12" skillet; add onions and 5 cups mushrooms. Sauté until onions are tender; add vegetable broth, pepper and dill weed. Bring to a boil; reduce heat and simmer, covered, for 15 minutes. Purée in small portions in a blender until smooth; return to skillet. Add remaining mushrooms; return to a boil. Reduce heat again; simmer, covered, 10 more minutes. Stir in milk and cream; heat without boiling until warmed. Serves 6.

Surprise friends & family by sending New Year's cards, wishing them well in the upcoming year...so thoughtful!

Cracked Wheat Bread

Jeff Doak
Delaware, OH

This bread makes an excellent sandwich...try toasting it and spreading with peanut butter too.

2 c. cracked wheat
1/2 c. brown sugar, packed
2 T. butter
1 T. salt

2 c. boiling water
2 pkgs. active dry yeast
1/2 c. warm water
5 to 5-1/2 c. all-purpose flour

Combine cracked wheat, brown sugar, butter and salt in a large mixing bowl; pour boiling water over mixture. Let stand until cooled to lukewarm. Sprinkle yeast over warm water in a small bowl; set aside for 10 minutes. Combine both mixtures; gradually blend in 4 cups flour. Turn out onto a floured surface; knead in enough remaining flour to make a stiff dough. Continue kneading for 8 to 10 minutes; place in a greased bowl, turning once to lightly coat all sides. Cover and let rise until double in bulk, about 1-1/2 hours; punch dough down. Divide into 2 loaves; place each loaf in a greased 8"x4" loaf pan. Let rise until double in bulk, about 1-1/4 hours. Bake at 400 degrees for 30 minutes. Makes 16 servings.

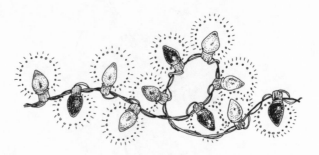

For a whimsical veggie tray, use mini cookie cutters to cut cucumber slices, zucchini and sweet peppers into merry munchies.

Cabbage Patch Stew

Linda Bernier
Scotland, CT

This hearty stew reheats easily and is just as tasty the next day.

1-1/2 lbs. ground beef
4 stalks celery, chopped
1 onion, chopped
7 c. cabbage, chopped
2 carrots, peeled and chopped
2 15-1/2 oz. cans kidney beans,
   drained and rinsed

28-oz. can diced tomatoes,
   undrained
3 c. beef broth
15-oz. can tomato sauce
1/2 t. sugar
pepper to taste

Brown beef with celery and onion over medium heat in a Dutch oven; drain and add remaining ingredients. Bring to a boil; reduce heat, cover and simmer until cabbage and carrots are tender, about one to 2 hours. Serves 6.

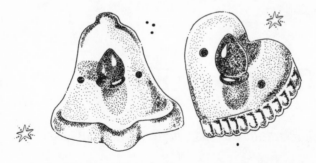

Enjoying dinner with friends? Make each place setting special by creating edible placecards...pipe garlic butter onto hearty wheat crackers and set a few at each setting.

Sour Cream-Dill Bread

Mary Beth Schlemmer
St. Petersburg, FL

This bread is so tasty alongside a hearty stew or pot roast.

3 c. biscuit baking mix
1-1/4 c. shredded Cheddar
    cheese
3/4 c. milk
1/2 c. sour cream

1 T. sugar
3/4 t. dill weed
3/4 t. dry mustard
1 egg

Stir all ingredients together until just moistened; spread in a greased 9"x5" loaf pan. Bake at 350 degrees for 45 to 50 minutes or until golden; cool in pan for 5 minutes. Remove from pan; cool completely. Makes 8 servings.

Cheddar Cheese-Garlic Biscuits

Joette Cole
Hudson, IL

Quick and delicious...perfect with any meal!

1/2 c. shredded Cheddar cheese
2 c. biscuit baking mix
1/2 t. garlic, minced

8 T. butter, melted and divided
2/3 c. milk
1/4 t. garlic powder

Combine cheese, biscuit mix and garlic; add 5 tablespoons melted butter and milk until just moistened. Drop by tablespoonfuls onto a lightly greased baking sheet; bake at 450 degrees for 10 to 12 minutes or until golden. Stir garlic powder and remaining melted butter together in a small bowl; brush on hot biscuits. Makes 12 to 16.

Sweet & Sour Stew

Karla Harrington
Anchorage, AK

This recipe was passed on to me by my grandmother, Tutu.
I like to serve it over wide egg noodles.

1/4 c. all-purpose flour
2 t. salt, divided
1/8 t. pepper
2 lbs. stew beef
1/4 c. oil
1 c. water

1/2 c. catsup
1/4 c. brown sugar, packed
1/4 c. vinegar
1 T. Worcestershire sauce
1 onion, sliced
3 carrots, peeled and sliced

Combine flour, one teaspoon salt and pepper together; add meat, tossing to coat. Brown meat in oil in a Dutch oven; reduce heat. Mix water, catsup, brown sugar, vinegar and Worcestershire sauce together; pour over meat. Add onion; cover and heat over low heat for 45 minutes. Stir in carrots; heat until meat and carrots are tender, about one to 1-1/2 hours. Serves 6.

I like days when feathers are snowing, and
all the eaves have petticoats showing.
- Aileen Fisher

Celebration Salad

Martha Yocom
Urbana, OH

Full of fruit and so fluffy!

14-oz. can sweetened condensed
  milk
8-oz. container frozen whipped
  topping, thawed
30-oz. can cherry pie filling
2 11-oz. cans mandarin
  oranges, drained

15-1/4 oz. can crushed
  pineapple, undrained
1 c. mini marshmallows
1/2 c. chopped nuts
Garnish: graham cracker crumbs

Blend milk and whipped topping together; add cherry pie filling. Fold
in remaining ingredients; spread into a serving bowl. Sprinkle with
graham cracker crumbs. Refrigerate before serving. Makes 10 to
12 servings.

Toast the new year in style!
Stick foil stars on beverage
glasses, then tie a length of
foil star garland or silvery
ribbon around the stem.

Creamy Waldorf Salad

Dot Duke
Raleigh, NC

For a low-fat version of this traditional salad, use non-fat yogurt, fat-free whipped topping and fat-free salad dressing.

3 c. apples, cored, peeled
   and chopped
1 T. lemon juice
1/2 c. celery, chopped
1/2 c. raisins
1/4 c. chopped walnuts

1/2 c. vanilla yogurt
1/2 c. frozen whipped topping,
   thawed
2 T. mayonnaise-type salad
   dressing
Optional: 1/2 t. lemon zest

Place apples in a large serving bowl; sprinkle with lemon juice. Add celery, raisins and walnuts; toss gently. Combine yogurt, whipped topping and mayonnaise-type salad dressing in another bowl; stir into fruit mixture until apples are well coated. Sprinkle with lemon zest, if desired. Makes 4 servings.

New Year's party hats are a great way to celebrate.
Shape heavy construction paper into a cone,
decorate with glitter, sequins, ribbon
and buttons...let the party begin!

Mixed Bean Salad

*Karen Shepherd
Elko, NV*

A welcome addition to any potluck!

16-oz. can cut green beans, drained
16-oz. can kidney beans, drained
15-oz. can garbanzo beans, drained
2-1/2 oz. can sliced black olives, drained
1/4 c. fresh parsley, chopped
1 c. oil

1/4 c. vinegar
2 T. onion, finely chopped
1 T. fresh basil, chopped
1-1/2 t. fresh oregano, chopped
1 t. sugar
1 t. dry mustard
3/4 t. salt
1/4 t. pepper
2 cloves garlic, minced

Combine beans, olives and parsley in a large bowl; set aside. Mix remaining ingredients together; pour over beans. Cover and refrigerate at least 3 hours; stir occasionally. Makes 6 servings.

To add a whimsical touch to meat and vegetable dishes, use
a mini cookie cutter to cut shapes from thinly sliced potatoes.
Sauté the potato shapes until golden and use as a crunchy garnish.

Cornbread Stuffing

Susan Harrison
Stillwater, OK

Serve alongside roasted chicken or turkey.

1 c. celery, chopped
1 c. onion, chopped
3 T. butter, melted
4 c. cornbread, crumbled

4 c. dry herb stuffing mix
1 c. giblets, cooked and chopped
dried sage to taste
2 10-1/2 oz. cans chicken broth

Sauté celery and onion in butter over medium heat; set aside. Combine cornbread, stuffing mix, vegetables and giblets; mix well. Spread mixture in a 13"x9" baking dish; sprinkle with sage. Moisten mixture with chicken broth; cover and bake at 325 degrees for 20 minutes. Uncover and continue baking another 10 minutes. Serves 6.

Small, blown-glass ornaments make excellent party favors.
Tie them onto napkin rings with colorful ribbon and
a tag that has each guest's name on it.

Cabbage Au Gratin

Barbara Giese
Spirit Lake, IA

*Serve with grilled pork chops in place of sauerkraut
to welcome in the New Year.*

2 c. cabbage, shredded
1/2 c. carrot, grated
1/4 c. green onions, chopped
1 egg
1/2 c. milk

1/4 c. shredded Swiss cheese
1/4 t. seasoned salt
1/4 t. fresh parsley, minced
1-1/4 T. shredded Parmesan
    cheese

Sauté cabbage, carrot and onion in a 10" skillet sprayed with non-stick vegetable spray; pour into a greased one-quart baking dish. Whisk egg and milk together in a small bowl; add Swiss cheese and seasoned salt. Pour over vegetable mixture; sprinkle with parsley and Parmesan cheese. Bake, uncovered, at 350 degrees for 30 to 35 minutes or until a knife inserted in the center removes clean. Makes 2 to 3 servings.

For a sparkly New Year's centerpiece, fill a pretty
glass punch bowl with water, sprinkle with silver glitter
and add several floating candles...delightful!

Festive Salads & Sides

Cheesy Potatoes

Karen Suvak
Galena, OH

So simple and scrumptious...better have the recipe on hand!

32-oz. pkg. frozen shredded
   hashbrowns, partially
   thawed
2 T. onion, chopped
2 c. Cheddar cheese, grated
2 c. sour cream

10-3/4 oz. can cream of chicken
   soup
1 t. salt
1/4 t. pepper
2 c. corn flake cereal, crushed
1/2 c. butter, melted

In a large bowl, combine all ingredients except for corn flake cereal
and butter. Mix well, place in a 13"x9" baking dish. In another bowl,
combine cereal and melted butter; sprinkle on top of potato mixture.
Bake, uncovered, at 350 degrees for one hour. Serves 10 to 12.

To make dinner rolls a little more special, brush the top of
each unbaked roll with a mixture of egg white and water,
then place a piece of flat-leaf parsley on top.
Brush again with the mixture and bake...so pretty!

Granny's Salad

Karla Durst
San Antonio, TX

*This recipe came from my husband's grandmother. We sometimes add
raisins, pineapple chunks or chopped apples for variety.*

2 c. elbow macaroni, cooked,
   drained and cooled
3 carrots, peeled and grated
3 to 4 bananas, sliced

1/4 c. sugar
1/2 c. mayonnaise-type salad
   dressing
salt and pepper to taste

Combine all the ingredients together; refrigerate until time to serve.
Serves 8 to 10.

Make nostalgic
gift tags from
vintage sheet
music found at
flea markets and
tag sales. Just cut
each sheet down to
the desired size and
glue a smaller piece
of plain cardstock
over it...so easy!

Cranberry Salad

Marylee Jensen
Tarpon Springs, FL

For a quick & easy dessert, top with cinnamon ice cream when serving...yum!

3 c. apples, cored, peeled
   and chopped
2 c. cranberries

2 T. all-purpose flour
1 c. sugar

Combine apples, cranberries and flour; toss to coat. Add sugar; mix well. Place in a 2-quart baking dish; sprinkle with topping. Bake, uncovered, at 350 degrees for 45 minutes; serve warm or cold. Makes 6 servings.

Topping:

3 pkgs. instant cinnamon-spice
   oatmeal
3/4 c. chopped pecans
1/2 c. all-purpose flour

1/2 c. brown sugar, packed
1/2 c. butter, softened

Combine all ingredients together in a mixing bowl; stir well.

Arrange sparkly vintage ornaments in a glass bowl for a simple holiday centerpiece.

Black Walnut & Wild Rice Supreme *Rita Morgan*
Pueblo, CO

This elegant side dish is perfect with chicken or pork...serve with a side of glazed carrots for a complete meal.

1 c. wild rice, uncooked
1/2 c. black walnuts
1 c. sliced mushrooms
1/2 c. onion, chopped

1/2 c. green pepper, chopped
4 T. butter, melted
2 t. garlic salt

Prepare wild rice according to package directions; set aside. Sauté black walnuts, mushrooms, onion and green pepper in butter for about 3 minutes or until the vegetables soften. Add wild rice and garlic salt; continue cooking, stirring several times, until rice is heated through. Serves 4 to 6.

Shimmering silver ribbon looks so pretty wound around a banister...look for wide ribbon with a decorative edge.

Butter Crumb Noodles

Gail Prather
Bethel, MN

This yummy side dish is quick to make and a family favorite.

8-oz. pkg. egg noodles, cooked
   and drained
3 slices whole-wheat bread
1/3 c. butter

1/4 c. fresh parsley, chopped
1/2 t. pepper
1/2 t. salt

Pour noodles in a serving bowl; set aside. Place bread in a blender; process until coarse crumbs form. Melt butter in a 10" skillet; add crumbs. Heat until golden; toss with noodles. Mix in parsley, pepper and salt; serve immediately. Makes 6 servings.

Fresh, shiny apples look so inviting in a
stoneware bowl on the buffet...wrap a homespun ribbon
around the bowl for a touch of country.

Homemade Chocolate Pudding

Kim Faulkner
Gooseberry Patch

Nothing beats the flavor of homemade chocolate pudding!

6 T. baking cocoa
3/4 c. sugar
2 T. cornstarch
1/4 t. salt

2 c. milk
1 egg, beaten
1-1/2 t. vanilla extract
2 T. butter

Combine first 4 ingredients together in a heavy saucepan over medium heat; add milk, stirring until thickened and bubbly. Heat and stir 2 minutes; remove from heat. Pour one cup mix in a bowl; quickly blend in egg. Mix back into cocoa mixture; heat and stir 2 more minutes. Remove from heat; stir in vanilla and butter. Pour into a serving bowl; cover surface with plastic wrap. Refrigerate without stirring until set. Serves 4.

Look back on all those cherished memories from the past year...keep a scrapbook of special events like new babies, weddings and family reunions and set it out when ringing in the new year.

Pretzel Salad

Lori Mulhern
Rosemount, MN

This tasty salad has just the right amount of crunch.

1 c. pretzels, crushed
1/2 c. butter, melted
1/2 c. plus 1/3 c. sugar, divided
8-oz. pkg. cream cheese,
    softened

20-oz. can crushed pineapple,
    drained
8-oz. container frozen whipped
    topping, thawed

Combine pretzels, butter, and 1/3 cup sugar; mix well. Spread on a baking sheet; bake at 400 degrees until golden and bubbly, about 6 minutes. Cool; break into pieces and set aside. Whip together cream cheese and remaining sugar; add pineapple. Gently fold in whipped topping; spread in a serving dish. Refrigerate; sprinkle with pretzel topping before serving. Serves 6 to 8.

Look for videos, CDs or tapes of New Year's concerts at libraries and rental stores...they're the perfect background music for a New Year's celebration!

New Year's Feast

Country Pork Tenderloin

Mary Murray
Gooseberry Patch

*The flavors of currants and rosemary blend for
a taste that is out of this world!*

2 t. salt
1/4 t. pepper
2-lb. pork tenderloin, trimmed
1 T. butter

1/2 c. red currant jelly
2 T. rosemary, crushed
1 c. whipping cream
2 T. all-purpose flour

Rub salt and pepper over pork; set aside. Melt butter in a 12" skillet;
add tenderloin; brown on all sides. Remove from heat; place tenderloin
in a roasting pan; spread top with jelly. Sprinkle with rosemary; bake
at 350 degrees for 40 minutes, basting once after 25 minutes. Whisk
cream and flour together; pour over roast. Bake for another 10 to
15 minutes. Serves 6.

Small cheer and great welcome make a merry feast!
-William Shakespeare

New Year's Feast

Tangy Country-Style Ribs

Kathy McLaren
Visalia, CA

We enjoy these ribs served with rice...try steamed white rice or a zesty pilaf.

4 lbs. boneless country-style
   pork ribs
1 onion, chopped
2 T. oil
1 c. chili sauce
1/2 c. water
1/4 c. lemon juice

2 T. brown sugar, packed
2 T. white vinegar
2 T. catsup
1 T. Worcestershire sauce
1/8 t. salt
1/8 t. pepper

Place ribs on a rack in a shallow roasting pan; cover and bake at 325 degrees for 30 minutes. While baking, sauté onion in oil until tender; add remaining ingredients. Reduce heat; simmer, uncovered, 5 minutes or until thickened. Drain ribs; brush with sauce. Bake, uncovered, for one to 1-1/2 hours; baste occasionally. Serves 8.

During New Year's dinner, ask everyone to share their best memory of the past year and what they're most looking forward to in the upcoming year.

Nacho Casserole

Barbara Sherman
Magna, UT

We enjoy this casserole with buttery cornbread
and applesauce for dessert.

1 lb. ground beef, browned
15-oz. can corn, drained
10-3/4 oz. can tomato soup
16-oz. can pork & beans

15-oz. pkg. nacho chips, broken
8-oz. pkg. shredded Cheddar
   cheese

Combine ground beef, corn, soup and pork & beans in a skillet; mix well. Heat until warmed through; spread into a 13"x9" ungreased baking dish. Cover with nacho chips; sprinkle cheese on top. Bake in a 350-degree oven until cheese is melted. Serves 6 to 8.

When serving a holiday buffet, be sure to label dishes
with table-tent cards so guests can easily see what
each is before they dig in.

Italian Casserole

*Stephanie Hunker
Fostoria, OH*

A golden biscuit top makes this hearty casserole a meal in itself.

1 lb. ground beef	2 c. shredded mozzarella cheese,
1/2 c. onion, chopped	divided
1 T. oil	9-oz. pkg. frozen mixed
3/4 c. water	vegetables, thawed
1/2 t. salt	2 12-oz. tubes refrigerated
1/4 t. pepper	biscuits
8-oz. can tomato sauce	1 T. margarine, melted
6-oz. can tomato paste	1/2 t. dried oregano

Brown ground beef in a 12" skillet with onion in oil; drain. Stir in
water, salt, pepper, tomato sauce, and tomato paste; simmer
15 minutes, stirring occasionally. Spread half the meat mixture into
a greased 13"x9" baking dish; sprinkle with 2/3 cup cheese. Spread
mixed vegetables evenly over cheese; top with 2/3 cup cheese. Spoon
remaining meat mixture on top; sprinkle with remaining cheese.
Separate each biscuit into 3 layers; arrange over hot meat mixture,
overlapping edges of 3 rows of 20 slices each. Gently brush with
margarine; sprinkle with oregano. Bake at 375 degrees for 22 to
27 minutes or until biscuits are golden. Makes 10 servings.

Provide a warm glow for holiday gatherings.
Set out fragrant candles in old-fashioned
canning jars tied with holiday ribbons.

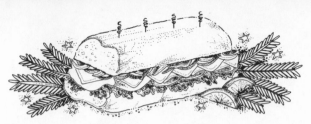

White Chicken Chili

Debi Perlaky
Northwood, OH

A delicious variation of a cold-weather classic.

1 onion, chopped
4-oz. can green chilies, chopped
2 10-1/2 oz. cans chicken
    broth, divided
1.25-oz. pkg. taco seasoning
    mix, divided
2 t. cayenne pepper
2 t. paprika

2 t. cumin
36-oz. jar Great Northern
    beans, drained
1 to 2 boneless, skinless chicken
    breasts, cooked and chopped
Garnish: sour cream and
    crushed tortilla chips

Sauté onion and green chilies with 1/3 cup chicken broth; add
3 teaspoons taco seasoning mix, pepper, paprika and cumin. Pour in
beans; mix in remaining broth. Bring to a boil; reduce heat. Add
chicken; simmer for one to 2 hours. Pour into serving bowls; garnish
with a dollop of sour cream and crushed tortilla chips. Serves 4.

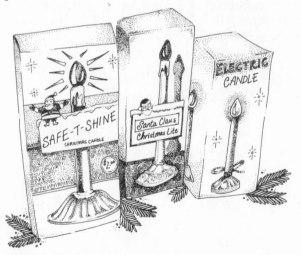

When serving specialty cheeses as an appetizer, unwrap and place
on a decorative serving tray one hour before the party begins...the
flavors are fullest when these cheeses are at room temperature.

New Year's Feast

Cajun Pecan Chicken

Delinda Blakney
Bridgeview, IL

Creamy mashed potatoes and hot, buttered corn are the perfect compliments to this spicy chicken.

1-1/2 c. pecan halves
1/3 c. bread crumbs
3/4 t. salt
3/4 t. paprika
1/2 t. dried oregano

1/2 t. pepper
1/2 t. cayenne pepper
1/2 c. buttermilk
3 to 4 bone-in chicken breasts
2 T. butter, melted

Combine first 7 ingredients in a food processor; process until nuts are chopped. Transfer to a plastic zipping bag; set aside. Pour buttermilk into a medium-size mixing bowl; dip chicken in milk. Place chicken in with spices, shaking to coat; arrange in a 13"x9" baking pan. Drizzle with butter; bake at 400 degrees for 30 to 40 minutes. Serves 6 to 8.

Liven up the party with a fun game! Have each guest write two silly resolutions on paper and drop them into a hat. Draw them out and have everyone guess who wrote each...the person with the most correct wins a prize!

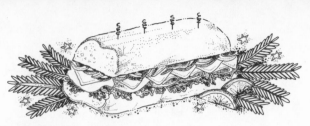

Barbecued Pork

Darrell Lawry
Kissimmee, FL

Serve as an open-faced sandwich on crusty bread...heaven!

1/3 c. plus 1 T. water
2/3 c. onion, chopped
1/2 c. carrots, chopped
1/4 c. catsup
2 T. vinegar
1 T. Worcestershire sauce
1 t. brown sugar, packed

1 t. chili powder
1/2 t. garlic powder
1/4 t. pepper
2 c. pork, cooked and
  thinly sliced
1/3 c. celery, sliced
2 t. cornstarch

Combine 1/3 cup water and next 9 ingredients together in a 4-quart saucepan; bring to a boil. Reduce heat; simmer, covered, for 10 minutes. Stir in pork and celery; simmer, covered, 5 minutes more. Whisk cornstarch with one tablespoon water; stir into meat mixture. Heat and stir until thickened and bubbly. Makes 4 servings.

Then sing, young hearts that are full of cheer, with never a thought
of sorrow; the old goes out, but the glad young year
comes merrily in tomorrow.
- Emily Miller

New Year's Feast

Pork Chops & Apples

Dale Duncan
Waterloo, IA

Melt-in-your-mouth pork chops are perfect
for holiday dinners and every day!

2 T. olive oil
4 pork chops
1 sweet onion, sliced
1/4 head red cabbage, sliced
1 Granny Smith apple, cored,
   peeled and sliced

1/4 c. cider vinegar
1 c. chicken broth
1/2 t. salt
1/4 t. pepper
2 t. caraway seed
1 T. sugar

Place a 13"x9" oven-proof pan in a 250-degree oven. Heat oil in a
large cast-iron skillet over medium-high heat until very hot. Add pork
chops and brown on both sides. Arrange in the oven-proof pan; cover
tightly with aluminum foil. Heat in oven for 14 minutes. Add onion to
skillet and heat over medium heat, stirring occasionally for 5 to
7 minutes or until soft. Mix in cabbage and apple; add vinegar. Using
a wooden spoon, stir well. Pour in chicken broth and heat until
cabbage is soft, about 6 minutes. Add salt, pepper, caraway seed and
sugar; stir to combine. Heat another 2 to 4 minutes. Spoon onto
serving plates; arrange pork chops on top. Makes 4 servings.

Instead of a traditional tossed
salad, set up a salad bar!
Bowls of favorite veggies and
crunchy toppers make a holiday
buffet even more fun!

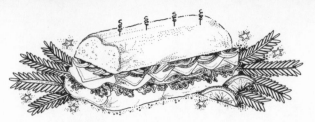

Raspberry-Orange Turkey

Liz Plotnick-Snay
Gooseberry Patch

This sweet & savory turkey is always a hit at our house!

3-lb. boneless turkey breast
1 c. orange juice
1 t. dried sage
1/2 t. dried thyme
1/2 t. pepper

salt to taste
1 t. orange zest
1-1/2 c. frozen raspberries
1/3 c. sugar

Place turkey breast in a 9"x9" baking pan; pour orange juice over the top. Sprinkle with sage, thyme, pepper, salt and orange zest. Roast at 350 degrees for 1-1/2 hours; baste occasionally. Combine raspberries and sugar in a medium-size mixing bowl; arrange around turkey breast and return to oven for 15 minutes. Let stand 10 minutes before slicing; serve spoonfuls of raspberries over slices. Serves 4.

Carrot curls make a colorful garnish! Cut long, thin strips with a vegetable peeler, roll up and secure with a toothpick. Soak in ice water for two hours...so easy!

Potato-Beef Casserole

Pat Obringer
Seven Lakes, NC

A variety of ingredients come together for a burst of flavor.

2 lbs. stew beef, cubed
2 onions, sliced
2 T. oil
water
2 potatoes, peeled and
  thinly sliced
10-3/4 oz. can cream of
  mushroom soup

1 c. sour cream
1-1/4 c. milk
1 t. salt
pepper to taste
1 c. shredded Cheddar cheese
1 c. potato chips, crushed

Brown beef with onions in oil; add one cup water. Heat until boiling; reduce heat, cover and simmer for one hour, adding additional water if necessary. Place meat in an ungreased 13"x9" baking pan; arrange potatoes over the top. Stir soup, sour cream, milk, salt and pepper together; pour over potatoes. Sprinkle with cheese and potato chips. Bake at 350 degrees for about 1-1/2 hours or until meat is tender. Serves 6.

To speed up party preparations, chop vegetables ahead of time. Place in plastic zipping bags and store in the fridge...they'll be ready to use when needed!

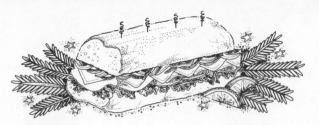

Easy Lasagna

Brenda Doak
Gooseberry Patch

We love this recipe...the noodles don't have to be boiled!

1 lb. ground beef, browned
1-1/2 T. Italian seasoning
32-oz. jar spaghetti sauce,
    divided
8-oz. pkg. lasagna noodles,
    uncooked

24-oz. container low-fat cottage
    cheese, divided
1 lb. mozzarella cheese, sliced
    and divided

Combine ground beef and Italian seasoning together; set aside. Pour
1/4 cup spaghetti sauce into a 13"x9" baking pan; tilt to cover.
Arrange a single layer of lasagna noodles over the sauce; spread half
the meat mixture and half the cottage cheese on top. Layer 1/3 of the
cheese slices over the cottage cheese. Add another layer noodles;
lightly cover with spaghetti sauce. Spread on remaining meat and
cottage cheese; layer 1/3 of mozzarella over the top. Add third layer
of noodles; pour on remaining spaghetti sauce. Cover tightly with
aluminum foil and bake at 350 degrees for one hour. Top with final
1/3 mozzarella cheese slices; replace foil and let stand 15 minutes
before serving. Makes 8 servings.

Turn vintage canning jars into party favors by filling them with
nuts or candy and tying with a colorful ribbon.

New Year's Feast

Slow-Cooker Sauerkraut & Pork

Amy Butcher
Columbus, GA

A quick & easy way to make a New Year's tradition.

20-oz. can sauerkraut,
   undrained
1/3 c. brown sugar, packed

1-1/2 lbs. ground pork sausage
1 onion, sliced

Combine sauerkraut and brown sugar in a medium mixing bowl; pour into a slow cooker. Arrange sausage and onion on top; heat on high for 2 hours, adding water if necessary. Reduce heat to low; heat for 2 more hours. Makes 4 to 6 servings.

Easy Pork & Sauerkraut

Lynda Robson
Boston, MA

A hearty halftime meal!

1-lb. pork roast, cubed
32-oz. jar sauerkraut, undrained
12-oz. bottle beer
1/2 apple, cored and peeled

1 T. clove garlic, minced
2 t. dill weed
1 t. onion salt
1 t. dry mustard

Combine all ingredients in a slow cooker; stir well. Heat on high for one hour; reduce heat to low and continue cooking for 5 hours or until pork is cooked through. Discard apple before serving. Serves 4 to 6.

Add a wreath of rosemary and some fresh rose petals or sparkly confetti around trays of appetizers and snack bowls. They'll brighten the presentation and the festivities!

Decadent Desserts

Our Favorite Cheesecake

Janet Moore
Roanoke, VA

I've had this recipe over 20 years...everyone loves it!

1-1/2 c. graham cracker crumbs
1/4 c. butter, melted
2/3 c. plus 2 T. sugar, divided
4 8-oz. pkgs. cream cheese,
    softened

1 t. vanilla extract
6 eggs
cinnamon to taste

Combine graham cracker crumbs, butter and 2 tablespoons sugar; press into the bottom of a lightly greased 10" springform pan. Bake at 350 degrees for 5 minutes; set aside to cool. Blend cream cheese until fluffy; add remaining sugar and vanilla. Cream mixture well; add eggs, one at a time, beating well after each addition. Pour into cooled crust; bake at 350 degrees for 40 to 50 minutes. Cool for 15 minutes. Spread on topping; sprinkle with cinnamon. Bake at 350 degrees for 10 more minutes; cool to room temperature. Refrigerate overnight up to 24 hours before serving. Makes 8 to 10 servings.

Topping:

2 c. sour cream
1 c. sugar

1 t. vanilla extract

Combine ingredients together; blend well.

Decadent Desserts

Chocolate-Coconut Sweeties

*Brenda Donley
Lake Isabella, MI*

This filled cookie is so tasty...they won't last long in the cookie jar!

1 c. margarine
1 c. powdered sugar
1/2 t. salt

1 t. vanilla extract
2-1/4 c. all-purpose flour

Cream margarine; add powdered sugar, salt and vanilla. Gradually blend in flour; shape dough into walnut-size balls. Using your thumb, gently make a depression in the center of each ball; place on ungreased baking sheets. Bake at 350 degrees for 12 to 15 minutes. Spoon a teaspoon of filling into each depression while warm; drizzle with frosting when cool. Makes 4 dozen.

Filling:

3/4 c. cream cheese
2 c. powdered sugar
4 T. all-purpose flour

2 t. vanilla extract
1 c. chopped walnuts
1 c. flaked coconut

Mix ingredients together well.

Frosting:

1 c. chocolate chips
4 T. margarine

4 T. water
1 c. powdered sugar

Heat chocolate chips, margarine and water in a double boiler until chips are melted; gradually whisk in powdered sugar until smooth and creamy.

Chocolate-Raspberry Fudge

Bobbi Lynne Wagner
Green Springs, OH

This decadent fudge is best when kept in the refrigerator.

14-oz. can sweetened condensed
   milk
3 c. semi-sweet chocolate chips

1-1/2 t. vanilla extract
1/4 t. salt

Line an 8"x8" baking pan with aluminum foil; cover with a layer of wax paper, overlapping any edges and set aside. Heat milk in a double boiler over medium heat for 3 to 4 minutes; gradually add chocolate chips. Stir constantly until melted and smooth; add vanilla and salt. Spread into prepared pan; cool to room temperature. Pour topping over fudge; refrigerate overnight. Cut into small squares to serve. Makes 3 dozen.

Topping:

1/4 c. whipping cream
3/4 t. raspberry extract

6-oz. pkg. raspberry chips

Heat cream in a heavy saucepan until just boiling; add raspberry extract, stirring to mix. Add raspberry chips; reduce heat to medium-low. Stir until chips are melted and mixture is smooth; cool to room temperature.

Add a wintry touch to a fruit
basket by poking small sprigs
of evergreen among the
fruits...finish it off with a
red velvet bow!

Decadent Desserts

Norwegian Cookies

Carla Nelson
Braham, MN

Enjoy these with a warm cup of coffee or tea in the comfort of family & friends.

1-1/3 c. plus 3 T. sugar,
   divided
1 c. plus 2 T. butter, softened
2 eggs
1 t. vanilla extract

3 c. all-purpose flour
1 T. baking powder
6-oz. pkg. semi-sweet
   chocolate chips
3/4 t. cinnamon

Blend 1-1/3 cups sugar, butter, eggs and vanilla together in a large mixing bowl; mix in flour, baking powder and chocolate chips. Divide the dough into quarters; roll each piece into a 15-inch rope on a lightly floured surface. Flatten slightly with a fork until about 1/2-inch thick; sprinkle with remaining sugar mixed with cinnamon. Bake on ungreased baking sheets at 350 degrees for 13 to 15 minutes; cut each roll diagonally into one-inch strips while warm. Cool before storing in airtight containers. Makes about 5 dozen.

Need butter softened in a hurry? Grate each stick with a cheese grater...it'll soften in minutes!

Date Pinwheels

Elaine Klenow-Klemm
East Tawas, MI

*This recipe was passed down to me from my
grandmother...it's a family favorite.*

1-1/3 c. chopped dates
1/2 c. sugar
1/2 c. water
1/2 c. chopped nuts
2/3 c. shortening
1-1/3 c. brown sugar, packed

2 eggs, beaten
2-2/3 c. all-purpose flour
1/2 t. salt
1/2 t. baking soda

Heat first 4 ingredients together in a saucepan, stirring until thickened;
set aside. Cream shortening until light and fluffy; add brown sugar
and eggs, mixing well. Sift flour, salt and baking soda together in a
separate mixing bowl; add to creamed mixture. Roll dough into
2 rectangles, 1/4-inch thick; spread with date mixture. Roll up jelly
roll-style; wrap in wax paper and refrigerate overnight. Slice and place
on greased baking sheets; bake at 375 degrees for 8 minutes or until
golden. Makes about 5 dozen.

A festive piñata adds instant fun to your fiesta! Look for new ones
in all shapes and sizes...fill with little surprises like
hard candy, small toys and confetti!

Decadent Desserts

Maple Memory Cookies

Jeanne Hodack
Norwich, NY

These simple drop cookies are perfect for sharing...pack them in a basket with some herbal tea and two mugs for a visit to a friend!

1/2 c. brown sugar, packed
3/4 c. shortening
1 egg
1 t. maple flavoring
2-1/4 c. all-purpose flour

2 t. baking powder
1/2 t. baking soda
1/2 t. salt
1/2 c. maple syrup
1/2 c. chopped walnuts

Combine first 4 ingredients together in a large mixing bowl; mix well. Stir dry ingredients in a separate mixing bowl; add into shortening mixture alternately with maple syrup. Fold in walnuts; drop by teaspoonfuls onto ungreased baking sheets. Bake at 400 degrees for 8 to 10 minutes. Makes 4 to 5 dozen.

Have fun counting down to the new year! Use number cookie cutters to cut appetizers, finger sandwiches and cookies...try mini cutters for cheese and veggies too.

Revel Bars

Michelle Campen
Peoria, IL

I remember making these twice a week as a teenager.

1 c. margarine	2-1/2 c. all-purpose flour
2 c. brown sugar, packed	1 t. baking soda
2 eggs	3 c. quick-cooking oats,
1 t. vanilla extract	uncooked

Mix together the first 4 ingredients; add dry ingredients. Spread
2/3 mixture in bottom of a greased 15"x10" baking pan; pour topping
over the top. Sprinkle with remaining oat and sugar mixture. Bake
at 350 degrees for 25 to 30 minutes; cool and cut into bars. Makes
2 dozen.

Topping:

12-oz. pkg. chocolate chips	2 T. margarine
14-oz. can sweetened condensed	2 t. vanilla extract
milk	1 c. chopped nuts
1 t. salt	

Combine chocolate chips, milk, salt and margarine in a heavy
saucepan; heat over medium heat, stirring until melted and smooth.
Add vanilla and nuts; mix well.

Add a sweet touch to holiday desserts with chocolate curls! Use a
vegetable peeler to slice thin strips of chocolate from a chocolate bar
and place them on top of cakes, brownies and frosted cookies.

Decadent Desserts

Quick Company Pineapple Pie
Elizabeth VanEtten
Warwick, NY

Use a wet knife to slice this light, refreshing pie when serving.

20-oz. can crushed pineapple,
   drained
4-oz. can mandarin oranges,
   drained
3-1/2 oz. pkg. instant lemon
   pudding mix

8-oz. container frozen whipped
   topping, thawed
9-inch graham cracker pie crust

Blend pineapple, oranges and pudding mix together until thickened;
fold in whipped topping. Spread into crust; refrigerate until firm, at
least 2 hours. Serves 8.

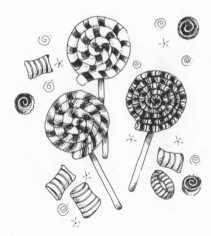

Brighten up gatherings with friends & family by stringing
sparkly white lights across curtain rods and
around entryways...simple and festive!

Chocolate-Berry Pie

Adrienne Payne
Omaha, NE

Serve with whipped topping or ice cream.

1 c. sugar
1/3 c. all-purpose flour
1 c. milk chocolate chips
2 c. blueberries
1 c. blackberries

1 c. raspberries
1 pear, cored, peeled and
   thinly sliced
2 9-inch refrigerated pie crusts

Combine sugar, flour and chocolate chips together; gently add berries, tossing to coat. Line bottom of one pie crust with sliced pears; spread berry mixture evenly over pears. Cover with second crust; flute edges and vent top. Bake in a 400-degree oven for 40 to 65 minutes or until golden. Cool slightly before serving. Makes 8 servings.

Make crystal-clear ice cubes...it's berry easy! Just boil water before
freezing, cool and drop raspberries or blueberries into ice trays.
Make oversized cubes for the punch bowl too. Just freeze
juice or water in muffin tins and pop out.

Decadent Desserts

Pistachio Cake

Ethel Bolton
Vienna, VA

A popular cake in the 1970's...it's still very good, easy to make and looks so festive!

18-1/2 oz. pkg. white cake mix
3.4-oz. pkg. instant pistachio
    pudding mix
1 c. oil

3 eggs
1/2 c. chopped nuts
1 c. club soda
Garnish: chopped nuts

Combine ingredients; blend for 4 minutes. Pour batter into a greased and floured 10" tube pan; bake at 350 degrees for 45 to 50 minutes or until toothpick inserted in center of cake removes clean. Cool in pan for 10 to 15 minutes; remove and cool completely on a wire rack. Frost and garnish with nuts; refrigerate until ready to serve. Makes 12 servings.

Frosting:

2 envelopes whipped topping
    mix
1-1/2 c. cold milk

3.4-oz. instant pistachio
    pudding mix

Combine whipped topping mix and milk together; blend until soft peaks form. Add pudding mix; blend until fluffy.

A "time"ly display!
Gather up little hourglasses,
wind-up alarm clocks and
kitchen timers...set them all
to go off at midnight.

Peanut Butter Candy Cakes

Kimberly McCarty
Goose Creek, SC

Forget about the resolutions...these are worth it!

2 c. sugar
3 T. oil, divided
1 t. vanilla extract
4 eggs
2 c. all-purpose flour, divided

1 c. milk
1 c. creamy peanut butter
8-oz. milk chocolate candy bar

In a large mixing bowl, blend sugar, 2 tablespoons oil, vanilla and eggs on high speed for 3 minutes. Reduce speed to low and add one cup flour, milk and remaining flour until combined. Increase speed to high and beat for 3 minutes. Batter will be very thin. Pour into a greased and floured 15"x10" lightly greased jelly roll pan. Bake at 350 degrees for 25 minutes. Cool cake for 10 minutes. Warm peanut butter until softened in a double boiler; spread over warm cake. Refrigerate until peanut butter hardens. Melt chocolate bar with remaining oil; spread over peanut butter. Refrigerate until chocolate hardens. Remove from refrigerator 10 minutes before serving. Cut into squares. Makes 48 servings.

Champagne glass candles are great party favors. Just suspend a wick in the center of a champagne flute and fill with melted wax...using a paint pen, personalize each with guest's name and the date!

Decadent Desserts

Nut Roll Bars

Shelly Schenkel
Sioux Falls, SD

Kids gobble up these rich and tasty treats.

18-1/4 oz. pkg. yellow cake mix
1/4 c. butter, melted
1 egg
3 c. mini marshmallows
10 to 12-oz. pkg. peanut butter
    chips

1/2 c. corn syrup
1/2 c. butter
1 t. vanilla extract
2 c. chopped peanuts
2 c. crispy rice cereal

Combine cake mix, melted butter and egg; press into a 13"x9" pan. Bake at 350 degrees for 10 to 12 minutes. Arrange marshmallows on top and return to oven for about 3 minutes or until marshmallows puff up. Melt chips, corn syrup and butter in a double boiler; stir in vanilla. Pour mixture over peanuts and crispy rice cereal, stirring to coat; spread evenly over marshmallow layer. Refrigerate and cut into bars. Makes 24.

May our house always be too small to hold all of our friends.
- Traditional New Year's Toast

Index

Index

snowballs gingerbread men glittering gumdrops ice skating sparkly tinsel yummy cookies rock'n around the Christmas tree candles glow dancing snowflakes Ho·Ho·Ho mom's apron woolly mittens